W9-BFS-022

ESSAYS ON THE PROPER PATH

A FAILURE LOOKS AT LIFE

By

Frank M. Manfredi

© 2002 by Frank Manfredi. All rights reserved.

No part of this book may be reproduced, stored in a
retrieval system, or transmitted by any means,
electronic, mechanical, photocopying, recording, or
otherwise, without written permission from the author.

ISBN: 1-4033-5912-1 (e-book)
ISBN: 1-4033-5913-X (Paperback)

This book is printed on acid free paper.

1stBooks – rev. 10/24/03

This book is dedicated to those I have hurt.

To my family, friends and victims,

I am sorry.

TABLE OF CONTENTS

INTRODUCTION VII

THE SPECTER OF EVIL 1

WHY DOES GOD PERMIT EVIL TO EXIST? 7

A SPECIAL RELATIONSHIP- MAN AND EVIL 12

WHERE WAS GOD ON 9/11, 12/7/41, OKLAHOMA CITY, ... 18

A LOOK AT RELIGION 22

A LOOK AT RELIGION - (PART II) 27

THE TOOLS 32

THE KEY 35

DEFINITIONS 42

WHAT IS YOUR IQ LEVEL? 47

THE DECISION MAKING QUANDRY 55

THE MORE THINGS CHANGE THE MORE THEY STAY THE SAME 61

THE DIVINE QUALITIES 69

MARRIAGE 75

HOW I SURIVIVED ATTICA 79

THE CRIMINAL JUSTICE SYSTEM 86

WHY DO GOOD PEOPLE DO BAD THINGS 94

WHAT HAPPENED TO ME 99

SO YOU SCREWED UP – NOW WHAT? 106

CAN YOU HAVE BOTH WEALTH AND INTEGRITY? 111

WHAT IS IT ALL ABOUT? 117

INTRODUCTION

*"He is truly wise who
gains wisdom from another's mishaps"*
Publius Syrus

Countless books have been written on success. Few, however, dwell on failure. While people may disagree on the meaning of a successful life, they have little difficulty in recognizing a dismal failure. After reading only a few pages of this book, I am sure you would agree that if the Guinness Book of World Records maintained a category for the world's greatest failure, I would certainly warrant serious consideration for the title. Personally, I choose to define a failure as one who has sinned against their talents. Sin I did. And it has led me to this book.

In June of 1971, I stood at the precipice of a successful career. I had just received a Juris Doctor degree and was scheduled to sit for the New York Bar exam in a month. Beside me stood my bride of a few months. Behind me were my parents beaming pride that their eldest had become the first in the family to reach such heights. Success was virtually ordained. Grammar school was finished on an accelerated basis. College succumbed to my efforts in three years under a special program that allowed pre - admission to law school. Once in law school, my marks were near the high of my class. I was even elected president of the Law School and awarded a complete scholarship for my efforts. On that graduation day, I received the Distinguish Military Graduate award from the ROTC program. No - failure was not an option.

That Sunday in June of 1971, as we stood on the parade grounds, I recall seeing the American Flag waiving. Some years later, I saw the flag waive again. This time from a cell overlooking the prison yard in B Block of Sing Sing Prison. That symbol of freedom and sacrifice that flew so proudly over the open parade ground on graduation day was now framed by the bars of my prison cell. It is hard to admit that it took, not one, but two periods of imprisonment for me to come to grips with the depth of my failure.

There was no way my life should have turned out this way. But I was unaware of the neurotic compulsions housed in my mind. Constantly denying my problems, I was blind to the errors of thought that led me to that cell. More important, I was oblivious to the hurt I caused those who gave me their trust and love. My downfall was not sudden. Slowly, I slipped downward, never realizing what was happening. I never saw it coming. There was plenty of warning, however. But I denied that I had any problem. I never imagined I could become a criminal. Certainly, I had some success. I was blessed with a wife and children. My law practice was growing. Respect and admiration flowed from those around me. Yet, like a cancer, slowly I destroyed my life until it was gone – all gone.

As I look back, I suggest that more can be gathered by looking at failure then by following the road taken by others to success. For the demons I fought and errors I made will surface in others. Statistics are on my side. There are far more failures than successes in our world. Our focus, therefore, should not be on what made the few rise to dizzying heights, but on what traits cause the many to fall.

I have put together this series of essays on questions that have troubled me. They contain glimpses of my personal life, and try to answer the questions raised by the problems of life. From my experience, a philosophy of the proper path in life has developed, and is offered for your consideration.

Perhaps no one will read a word I have written. Yet, if during a period of personal crisis, one individual seizes upon my words and quells the turmoil, then I have helped. Or if one of my thoughts helps someone avoid the road to self destruction, then there is benefit.

But why be concerned with my musings at all? Certainly, what can be gained from listening to a felon, a defrocked lawyer, a liar, thief, and cheat? What could I offer anyone seeking a fulfilling, prosperous, successful life? Unfortunately for me, I have had a tremendous amount of time to reflect on life. In fact, my first notes were recorded while in solitary lock down, a 23 hour a day confinement caused by a purported disciplinary infraction. Just as a boomerang always returns to the thrower, I have always returned to the important questions raised in these essays. You must remember, though, that a boomerang only returns when it misses the target. If it succeeds in its mission, there is no need to return. Although I have had many opportunities, I have never come close to the target of a successful life. And so like that failed boomerang, I return to some fundamental questions.

My answers are not meant to be definitive. I know I have not solved the mysteries of existence. All of the questions raised have received vast intellectual treatment. And yet, they still are unanswered. I seek; only, to provoke some thoughts on questions we normally shirk because of the pressures of our daily life.

Victor Hugo wrote in Les Miserables that ignominy thirsts for respect. Hugo's hero Jean Valjean finally found his respect, not in fame or fortune, but in the human quality of love. But unlike Valjean, to date, I have not been privy to such redemption. So perhaps, this effort is my attempt to quench my thirst.

THE SPECTER OF EVIL

"To live without evil belongs only to the gods."
Sophocles

A thirteen-year-old boy grabs a gun, points the muzzle, and within mere moments ends the lives of his mother and father. The thirst for death unsatisfied, he travels to his high school and starts firing. The sounds of teens playing in the yard soon turn to screams of pain and shock. Four youths lie dead, and immediately the airwaves are full of denunciations, while psychological experts proffer their explanations for these actions.

By any definition, these inexplicable, unjustifiable actions, with the resulting loss of life qualify as the essence of evil. What demons or thoughts must have filled that boy's mind before he killed his own parents and four of his friends? Six futures suddenly severed by the hands of one so young.

Within hours, on the other side of the globe, two pieces of rock far below the surface move ever so slightly. That shift along a fault line causes a tremor shaking the ground; hence an earthquake. These few moments of seismic terror crush a village in a third world country. When the earth finally settles there are five thousand men, women and children dead. Countless more missing. Is not such a result just as evil as the first example?

The question of why there is evil in the world, and the role of God, if any, in combating or creating this nefarious force has always mystified thinkers. I can picture our primitive ancestors sitting around a fire, grunting to one another, bemoaning the death of their friend "Og" killed for no apparent reason by their good neighbor "Mog".

But in addressing this issue, there appears to be a disturbing inconsistency. We lament the evil wrought upon

1

man by man, but ignore or attempt to differentiate the evil caused to man by the forces of nature. Any theory or explanation of the concept of evil must address both scenarios. For despite the vast numbers of humans senselessly killed, tortured or maimed by man, the total pales when compared to the death and suffering caused by the forces of nature.

The various theories for evil compiled over the centuries fill countless volumes of deep philosophical and theological thought. Is evil the result of the action of a specific entity embodied in the concept of Satan? Or is evil merely the absence of good? Perhaps it is the existence of the demon or bad seed? Maybe, the mystery is the result of the falling away from God by Man; the original sin? It could be God's will, or the result of Man's free will. Or it could exist without any supernatural intervention, and be the result of psychiatric disorder. Each of these concepts has been offered at various times as an explanation for evil in the world.

The problem is that these explanations can be applied to one type of evil, such as that wrought upon man by man, but they fail to explain the death and destruction caused by nature. While I can comprehend, for example, Satan possessing the soul of a person, causing an individual to commit the most terrifying of acts, I cannot accept the very same Satan inhabiting the inanimate Earth causing nature's turmoil. Mindless death and destruction is evil. There is no justifiable distinction between the ravages caused by man, and the tragedies created by nature.

And what of the role of God in either creating or permitting this disorder. Troublesome questions indeed. From our personal experiences with pain and suffering perhaps there is a clue to the answer.

For a parent to bury a child is the greatest of sorrows. The tragedy is magnified when the child is young. I can still see the small, white coffin where one of my cousins laid. He was named Sam, after his father. The boy, one of a set of twins, had been in all respects healthy.

Suddenly, for no reason, an infinitesimal microbe invaded the boy's body. The bacteria have a name, and so to does the disease - spinal meningitis. A fever developed. Not unusual for a young boy. The temperature rises, pain in the neck and head increase, and in 48 hours – death.

I hear, even now, the voice of the boy's father crying that he should never have named his son after him. Nothing but bad luck would follow, he sobbed. In the funeral home, one group of mourners cursed God. Another section praised the power and will of the Almighty in calling the youngster back to its side.

The loss of this boy's life was just as senseless whether caused by a microbe or mass murderer. Deaths attributable to disease over history far exceed the devastation created by the most prolific of human murderers. Senseless, tragic, cruel, untimely death by whatever the cause is wrong. It is the epitome of evil.

What happened to my cousin was as simple as it was tragic. A minute organism created by the very same forces that gave rise to our own complex bodies was acting in full accordance with its nature. In invading this host body, the microbe did not particularly choose one boy over another. It did not intentionally seek to injure or take a life. No, the ability to intentionally injure or kill is reserved for the nature of the highest of animals – man. One organism, the microbe, acting in accordance with its own nature; its own need to survive conflicted with the other organism; that of the boy. In this instance, because the immune system of the lad failed to respond satisfactorily the microbe grew and the boy died.

Our universe was created from randomness and chaos. Infinite conflict between various forms of matter and energy formed our planet and our existence. Whether there is a divine plan to this phenomena will be discussed later. But

3

for us, pain and suffering is the result of such conflict. As nature shows, this conflict if properly channeled can result in growth. The forces of nature act blindly to create death and destruction of life forms. From the conflict and chaos, tragedy often results. If in doubt, just talk with any dinosaur about the climatic calamity that resulted in their extinction. Different life forms seeking to fulfill their inherent nature will conflict. Randomly, chaotically and death results.

Clearly, the evil of nature is a result of the conflict between various forces and life forms. Even the shifting earth that caused the earthquake was acting according to its nature. Changing, growing and acting with randomness. But what of man? Being in prison, I have seen the face of evil. I have looked into the eyes of some men, and viewed the stare that hides a deep frightening force. These are prisoners who have committed the most brutal, reprehensible acts. Some even receive pleasure from recalling the events. And frightfully, many would commit similar acts again, if society were to afford them the opportunity. Ironically and fortunately, the number of prisoners that fall into this special evil category is not as high as the politicians would have us believe.

Throughout the State, legends have been structured around the most notorious of these prisoners. Ron DeFeo is just such a person. Having killed his mother, brothers and sister in a night of terror, he would often emphasize the truth of any of his prison conversations by swearing on the graves of his dead family. Frightening, since he created these graves. His acts spawned the moniker "Amityville Horror." Books and movies followed seeking to mystify and supernaturalize the events. To be sure, questions remain unanswered about the murders. Why was no one wakened by the shots that had to occur at different times since the bodies were found on different levels of the house? Why did the dog fail to bark? Why did no one see the lights on in the house?

Ron's own version of that night has evolved over the years. Initially, he proffered a mob rubout theory. Then, during his trial, insanity was the defense. This gave rise to the evil possession rumors. Recently, he admitted killing his sister to stop her from turning the weapon on him. After, of course, his sister shot the others.

Ron is a strange person. I know that is understatement. He works out daily with an animal like ferocity. He constantly yells and complains about one prison official or another. The Courts, State, Suffolk County District Attorney or his wife are his favorite targets. Yes, his wife. In my travels in the prison system, I am amazed at how the most notorious and vicious of men have no difficulty in obtaining female companionship. The attraction escapes me. But in this essay, I am trying merely to unravel the mysteries of the universe. I leave the workings of a women's mind and heart to a far more courageous soul.

The endless and intense complaining by Ron does not trouble his fellow inmates. We recognized that it is his "tool"; his means to survive. Ironically, inside of the man lies a generous, warm streak. Countless times he would give clothing, coffee or food to an inmate who is without. All done anonymously. But there were moments when his eyes would fixate in what I can only describe as a Charles Manson like stare. The emptiness and depravity of what he did, and what, I believe, he is still capable of doing shines through.

One aspect of the Ron DeFeo legend involves Green Haven Correctional Facility. Smack in the middle of the darkness and irrationality that is maximum security confinement lies a touch of beauty, St. Paul's Chapel. The chapel, the home of many inmate activities, is on a plot of well-tailored grass within the walls. Surrounding the structure are several ponds stocked with gold fish and turtles. In the warm months, a fountain sprays water high in the air over the ponds.

For years, the chaplains have attempted to guide Ron back to the Church. I imagine such a return would guarantee the successful priest a position of Cardinal or at the least a Bishop designation. Ron started to bend to the pressure. One day, he exited the prison hallway, and walked on the grass stopping a few feet before the Church doors. He looked up at the cross atop the structure, and announced to his fellow prisoners that he could not go on. He turned, and left. Not returning since.

That night, twenty gold fish mysteriously died in the pond. The deaths were made all the more strange when you realize that the symbol for Christ in the early days of the church was the fish. Thus, the rumor of the Anti-Christ being alive and well in Green Haven prison flourished.

The issue of evil in man centers on defining the nature of the beast. Man is the only animal capable of acting with a conscious reason and purpose. Although the extent of man's consciousness is not fully understood, we know man can think. Whether instilled by supernatural design or evolutionary forces, he has the trait of free will. He can choose to act or not. But where does the evil come from?

WHY DOES GOD PERMIT EVIL TO EXIST?

"Good and Evil are God's Prejudices."
Nietzsche

"Whoever admits that anything living is evil must either believe that God is malignantly capable of creating evil, or else believe that God has made many mistakes in His attempt to make a perfect being."
George Bernard Shaw

Somewhere on the far side of the planet Jupiter two boulders traveling in opposite directions, both trapped in orbit around the most massive planet of our system, randomly collide. One of these pieces of rock, the smaller one, only 100 yards circular, careens away from the planet free after centuries of circling purposelessly. This mindless object is thrown on a new course. Into the vast darkness of space, there is a blue dot miles away. That dot, of course, is Earth. The rock picks up speed as the gravitational force of the sun dutifully performs its function.

Our telescopes notice the occurrence. At first, the rock, now called a meteor, is dismissed as just one of the many millions that fly by the earth on a routine basis. But quickly computers start spitting out projections on the course and the scientists announce that there is 95% likelihood that the meteor will strike our planet. Worse they project a 75% chance that the rock will hit right in the heart of Miami, Florida. The potential death toll is well into the millions, and the devastation to Florida and the atmosphere of the planet cannot even be analyzed.

Not to worry, soon after the announcement buses of people start filling the area. Millions of Christians of all denominations start kneeling in fervent prayer. Certainly, the hand of Jesus the Savior would not permit such destruction. Of course, countless Muslims join them all prostrate facing the East, valiantly asking for the intervention of Allah to save his children. Not to be undone, those of the Jewish faith seek the intervention of Yahweh for protection. Somehow a miracle is expected. The hand of God should come and flick away this mere stone. Certainly it has the power. It created this universe. The meteor must bend to the Creator's will.

What will happen? There will be no sudden right turn for this stone. God will not intervene. The rock is destined to crash on the community killing those engaged in the most fervent prayer. That meteor is about to cause an evil act. But the story has a happy ending. For at the same time the masses are engaged in prayer, one scientist computes an interception formula, and successfully launches a missile to slightly deflect the stone off the course. Harmlessly, it bounces off the atmosphere of the earth. Is the story far fetched? No indeed. The dinosaurs, who once ruled the earth, were decimated when just such a stone that landed somewhere in the Mexican continent.

All these objects are a result of the creation. They are all performing according to their nature. The stone that is plummeting to earth is acting in full accord with the laws of physics. So too, is the sole scientist by using the rational brain, and computing the intercept course, acting in accord with nature.

Here is the point. There is no guarantee. Try as one might, the scientist could have made an error. After all, mistakes are part of what makes us human. The missile could have been too late, even by a millisecond. Death and destruction would follow. There would have been no direct intervention by God. That hasn't happened since the ancient days of the Old Testament.

So why then does the Creator permit evil to exist in this universe, whether caused by nature or man? Why would God permit countless people to be destroyed by a piece of rock no larger then a football field? Just as confusing is why would the Creator permit one man to kill even one innocent, let alone the millions destroyed by man over the centuries?

We must, of course, assume the existence of God for the purpose of this discussion. If there is no God then we have no problem. All things would operate in accordance with their nature, and randomness and chaos assist in creating the unsatisfactory results. Further, we must also assume that this Creative Force that brought this universe into existence from nothingness is an all-perfect entity. Pure creativity, and I argue, pure love are integral parts of the nature of this Creator. Unfortunately, there are limits to our knowledge. Our senses fail us when we try to comprehend such a Force. We can only discuss, or compute formulas concerning the "big bang" theory of existence. But to understand the force that brought all matter, space and time into existence within nanoseconds would overload the circuits of our finite brain. We are still struggling with the "how" of the universe; let alone the "why".

Yet, as humans in acting in furtherance of our rational nature, we try to unravel these questions. We tear open the smallest parts of an atom. We learn about electromagnetic force, the strong force, and the weak force. We compute the various spins on quarks. All in an attempt to unravel the secrets of the universe. It seems, though, the more we uncover, the more questions remain. The more we seek to deny the existence of this creative force, the more we uncover its probability.

The creation legends of antiquity indicate that at one time man lived in a near state of perfection. Then mankind did something to pull away from the majesty of the creator. The Adam and Eve story is just such an allegory. These

9

tales, however, are just early man's attempt to explain the pain and suffering in the world. God could not be responsible. It must be the fault of mankind. So reasoned the authors of Genesis and other creation epics. But evil need not be the sole responsibility of man.

I suggest that the answer lies, in part, upon definitions. We are taught that the Creator is all everything - all perfect, all loving, all forgiving, and all knowing. If one assumes that such a perfect, powerful force created the entire universe, then what type of environment could such a force create?

Could perfection create perfection? To do so means that the perfect creative force would be able to create itself. This could not be. Everything created by this force is less then perfect. The creative force is infinite. Therefore, the creation is finite. The creative force is all loving. Therefore, the creation must lack some love. The creative force is pure goodness. Therefore, the creation must lack some degree of goodness. The all-perfect creator must retain perfection to its self. The imperfections in our universe and in our very existence are a by-product of the creative process itself. The creative process has created a finite existence that on this plane of existence permits pain, suffering and evil to be part of our reality. Any other explanation would mean that the all-perfect creative force would have re-created itself. I argue that is not possible.

Perhaps we may be concerned about degrees. Dear God, we did not need this much evil in the universe. But once we accept the possibility that the results of creation are less then all perfect (for that state is reserved solely for the Almighty) then evil exists. And as a force in the universe it can act with the randomness, chaos and in accord with its own nature.

The question now becomes even more difficult. Okay, the universe is finite and hence, imperfect. Therefore, evil is a by-product of the creative act. Fine, but why can't God intervene on a daily basis to lessen the impact of this creative flaw? The Creator can, and does, but in ways foreign to us.

A SPECIAL RELATIONSHIP-
MAN AND EVIL

"Don't look forward to the day you stop suffering,
Because when it comes you know you're dead."
Tennesse Williams

Any cogent attempt to come to grips with evil in the world must resolve the suffering caused by nature upon man as well as the destruction created by man upon his brethren. All items in nature whether inanimate, or the simplest of life forms are endowed with certain properties. They respond to certain laws of physics. Thus, due to randomness or chaos they come in conflict with each other. The resultant change can caused death and destruction. The lifeless rock that comprised the fault line between two continents is responding to the uniform laws of nature contained in Newton's Laws of Gravity. When the rock slips it has no way of knowing that a few miles above a village of 5000 is destined for instant destruction.

A brick that falls from the top of a 10-story building is following these same laws. The brick does not know whether it will strike a Mother Theresa or a mafia hit man on the way down. But strike it will, and randomly cause death. All the while it is following the laws of nature. Clearly, the evil in nature is caused by this conflict of things acting in accordance with their own nature. But what of man? We are the only beings on earth that "know" what we are doing. Does a separate rule of evil cover our actions? I think not. Humans act in accordance with their own peculiar nature. Add to the equation conflict and randomness, and evil results.

What is man? At the deepest levels we are still primarily an animal. We contain a limbic base to our brain that retains our earliest instincts from the days we slivered or crawled our way to two feet. Our need to eat, procreate, and survive are the deepest drives. Somewhere along the way, our frontal lobes developed and our ability to have rational thought was a result. Mysteriously, consciousness was added to our being. For this discussion, it is not necessary to determine whether this human development resulted from Divine intervention or evolutionary forces. But conscious we are. And within our own being there is conflict. Whether one agrees with Freud or not, there can be no doubt that on the question of conflict, he was correct. The subconscious is in conflict with the conscious, and according to Freud, the super ego sees all between the two forces and punishes or rewards our behavior.

Man's very nature, therefore, is the combination of various conflicting forces. We possess a cool rational brain; yet are unable to control the deep emotion urges born from our animal days. We constantly demonstrate a proclivity to search out the pleasurable and avoid the pain of life. We inflict the most heinous of acts upon our neighbors, and then go home to kiss our children and lovingly pet the dog. Man's nature is the most complex of creations. Why then does man hurt man?

Simply, humans act according to our nature. We use free will to try and resolve the conflict that exists in our mind. And if causing death and destruction is the by product of this conflict resolution, then so be it. Let me be specific about the type of person we are talking about. Countless people fill the prisons of our world. Most are not evil. Most ills are caused by good people who have done bad things. If I question prison inmates, and I did, as to whether they were "good" people or not, only a handful would admit that they should be locked away. So I am not speaking about this large group, but of those we consider truly evil – the Hitlers, Mansons, Dahmers, Bin Ladens. People who seek destruction for destruction's sake.

Before I go further with this essay, there is a caveat. It involves the concept of the "evil seed". Religious doctrine teaches that evil, as an entity exists on a separate level. And from time to time, this force can invade human existence or control behavior from a distance. This belief is the basis for exorcisms, and is the foundation of many religious teachings on evil. I am not prepared to embrace this explanation. For as stated, I believe the evil caused by man upon man must be explained by the same concepts that permit evil in nature to wreak havoc. On a rational basis, however, I am troubled by this possibility.

We know that reality exists on several levels. As you read the words printed on this page, there appears to be an empty space between the eyes and the paper. We know this is not the case. Innumerable things exist in the space. They are simply too small to register on our senses, and thus appear non-existent. In this emptiness, all forms of radio waves travel freely as we read. Television waves, wireless communication fills that space. Atoms, molecules, and on a quantum level photons and quarks pulsate in and out of existence as I quietly read.

Even though, these objects escape our recognition, we know they are there. Not only do they exist we can create these objects; affect their patterns and even end their very existence. Those living on our plane of existence can interact with the particles and waves existing on this invisible plane below us. What a leap of intellectual ego is required to state with certainty that man is the highest level of existence in our universe. Cannot another plane exist, a higher plane, unknown to our senses, and as of yet unproven by our expanding, but still limited empirical knowledge? Further, if we can affect our lower plane with ease, why cannot this higher plane also interact with man, and affect our actions.

I am not willing to deny the existence of this higher plane. In fact, I believe fully that it does exist and can interact with humans, but it does not contain a separate, foreign evil, satanic force. The contents of this higher plane will be discussed in a subsequent essay, but suffice to say it exists at a level closer to perfection then we, and its interference in our lives has to do with the essence of consciousness. To explain away the horrors of man, by invoking outside forces is not intellectually honest. Remember, no such invocation is required to explain the disasters caused by nature upon man. Why then is it necessary to use this device to explain the actions of nature's finest creature?

Humans are flawed. Despite the complexities of the rational mind, and the mystical link contained in our subconscious, these developments are too new to control our actions. Man is pulled towards our base desires. Pleasure and fear are still the primary movers for action. Power is a recent development, but that desire also stems from pleasure seeking. The rational mind must be trained to accept certain values. The base instincts, for example, know nothing about the sanctity of life. And if the rational mind is devoid of a value system or adopts a system that is less then civilization dictates, our base instinct will seep through and control our action.

I have no doubt that Hitler feared, albeit irrationally, the Jews. Their death was a device to assuage that fear. I am sure that his anger at the Jews for the state of Germany's existence was likewise a result of fear. I also have no doubt, that he felt pleasure exhibiting the power necessary to carry out these monstrous orders. Pleasure, fear, anger and the resultant power all flow from our animal instinct unchecked by any value system assimilated by the rational mind. This evil then is caused by our nature, the conflict between our emotions and an underdeveloped rational mind.

Is not war the greatest of evils? Waves of humans destroying each other upon the commands of our governmental states. All war stems from the depths of our animal instinct. Territorial concerns, prejudices festered by religion or race, economic needs, land grabbing have decimated humankind from the time we dared to consider ourselves civilized. Some may argue that World War II was a war for values, good against evil, freedom against fascism, but the roots of that conflict lay in the territorial concerns and racial prejudices so evident in our primate ancestors. Unfortunately, at this stage of our development war is unavoidable. All civilizations have not developed the same value system, and many societies are still motivated in substance by religious, racial, and economic considerations.

The concept of Civil Disobedience is very illustrative on this point. Undoubtedly, Martin Luther King, and Mahatma Gandhi changed the world when they embraced the thoughts of Emerson portrayed in his essay on the ability of society to peaceably disobey an unjust law. The work of these two leaders, however, was successfully only because of the societies they sought to change. The United States and England, by and large, value human life. They find it difficult to fire into unarmed crowds. If the cause is just, then civil disobedience may work in these societies. Try the same tactic in China, however, as did the students in Tianneman Square, and death is the result. Why? - Because the societal values are different. What works in America or England fails in China.

Would the precarious balance of nuclear power that kept the peace by creating a mutual destructive deterrent have worked with other countries that did not in some way value human life? Fortunately for the world, the old USSR was concerned about the consequences of mass destruction, and the loss that would have taken place on their continent. Would nuclear weapons in the hand of a small country without the same value structure create the same type of breaking mechanism?

I wish I could state with certainty that the values of America will win out. I have my concerns. The vast numbers of the rest of the world that live in poverty, harboring deep anger could easily destroy our society. We know on a day-to-day basis that our emotions often win out over the rational part of our existence. Who can say whether the dark forces of our emotions cannot win on a large worldwide scale? There is no guarantee that Man will constantly evolve into a more civilized, just society. Darwin did not rule out a side step or a regression to what we once were. I am frightened when I look at our historical roots. Our government was fashioned in substantial part on the Roman Republic. But despite the Pax Romana, the peace brought upon the world by the Romans, that government fell. There is a time for all things. That government fell when a combination of outside attacks met with a crumbling moral structure. The so-called dark ages ensued. In the cyclical tides of history, when we are on the brink of great advancements in science, technology, and medicine, are we facing yet another dark age of more devastating consequence then in the past? The possibility is too real to be dismissed.

Perhaps the answer to these deep, dark questions is simple. Nature moves in accordance with its purposes and natural law. If death results from this conflict, that is the way of our existence. So too, do humans move in accordance with their nature. The conflict between the forces housed in our mind often results in victory for the animal in us. The result is evil.

Now for the hard question – What is the role of God in all this chaos?

17

WHERE WAS GOD ON
9/11, 12/7/41, OKLAHOMA CITY,
BLACK PLAGUE, ETC., ETC., ETC.

"But there are dreams that cannot be
And there are storms we cannot weather"
Les Miserables (the play)

"The Courage to Be is rooted in the God who appears
when God has disappeared in the anxiety of doubt."
Paul Tillich

As I mentioned previously, no greater evil exists then war. We recognize that fact, and yet, are unable to live in peace. As I write these words, I think about the first three days of July, 1864 when two armies met in Gettysburg, Pennsylvania. Two vast forces fought with savage brutality – brother against brother, American against American. Each army praying to God. Every soldier, I am sure, begging the Almighty for protection and victory against the other side. By the end of the third day, the South retreated. The Army of the Potomac was too weary to pursue. Over 50,000 men lay dead, wounded or missing. 50,000 of America's youth gone. And where was God?

Another famous military man proffered an answer to that very question. Napoleon Bonaparte once said that, "God is on the side of the Army with the largest reserve." Ironically, Napoleon would feel the wrath of the fickle hand of fate. Or was it the hand of God? Victor Hugo in Les Miserables devotes a section of this work to a stirring recital of the Battle of Waterloo. By all accounts, Napoleon should have been the victor that day. His strategy was sound, if not brilliant. His manpower was more then adequate. But even Hugo in his summary of the battle questions if there was more at work in this defeat. Napoleon wanted to attack Wellington first before the Prussians had an opportunity to join with the British against him. Having defeated the British, the French would turn against the Prussians and complete victory would be Bonaparte's.

But it rained that morning, delaying Napoleon's attack by a mere few hours. That delay permitted the Prussians to join the battle at the precise instant when victory was within the grasp of the French. Was it shear coincidence that the Prussian guides found the only route available to rush to the scene of battle, while the additional French troops so needed by Napoleon were hopelessly lost in the same terrain? Hugo wondered what changed history that day. Perhaps the fates determined that the era of Napoleon had lasted long enough, and it was time for civilization to move on. Was it just an example of the hand of God at work?

Hindsight permits ample instances of good fortune in battle. The course of history has turned very often on the weather, coincidence or just dumb luck. Yet, I find it difficult to accept the view that God sits and roots for one army against another, regardless of how just the cause. Lincoln addressed this question with somber poetry in his Second Inaugural Address. The ancient Greeks created the picture of the Gods actively involved in their lives to help cope with the difficulty in explaining random results. So was it the hand of God that steered the United States airplanes to find the Japanese aircraft carriers at the Battle of Midway that led to a miraculous victory? Was it the protective force of the Almighty that made you swerve in time to avoid that collision with an on coming car?

The way of our existence makes it clear that God does not interfere on this plane of reality. The question is not whether the Creative force has the power to suspend the laws of nature. The question rather is what are the total laws of nature. On our plane of finite existence, growth and change are the result of conflict. That is the reality. But on that higher plane of existence, the one we know exists when we close our eyes and engage in deep prayer, something else happens. Part of the total laws of nature involves this higher plane of existence. And it is on this higher plane, that the force that is God affects our daily existence. No, God will not flick away an oncoming bullet to save our life. The strength, and the tools to survive however, will flow from that higher plane, and that strength, often called spirituality fills our very consciousness.

Mankind is more than a rational, calculating computer. We are more than a feeling, emotional throwback to our ancestors instincts of fight or flight. Some characteristics seem to flow from a higher source. Courage, for example, is the ability to act in the face of fear. It is not derived from our rational side, since much of what we do with courage is not rational. Nor does it flow from the animal, emotional side of our existence. It is as though we can act in accord with a higher purpose.

Our own creative ability seems to follow this higher purpose. The creative impulse appears to flow from outside our very being and fills both the rational and emotional side of our nature. Love is more than an evolved state of animalistic caring. That gift serves a higher purpose, and for many of the great thinkers love constitutes the meaning and purpose of human life. It is on this level that the invisible, all pervasive creative, loving force that is God fills all aspects of this universe. While the creative force operates on all planes of existence, on this finite level, it does not change the laws of physics. On the higher level, it operates to create the very essence of what makes us human.

On this level, humans suffer. On the higher level, we love, we create, we care, we act with courage; we are truly human. God does recognize the suffering of humans. One of the fundamentals of Christian religion is the suffering God in Jesus Christ. The Son of God underwent the pain of this finite level to reveal the wonders of the higher existence. God was there on September 11. God was there at Pearl Harbor. The Creator was there when the countless innocents were buried as a result of the Black Plague. Present, as well, when the children died at Oklahoma City.

And God was there on the battlefields of Gettysburg. Not as a participant. Not rooting for one side against the other. But present in the words of Lincoln, during his address, when our President rededicated our country to the principles of freedom so beautifully contained in the Declaration of Independence. God is there in every act of creative love, every act of courage, every act of growth. Every time we as humans increase our knowledge, care and struggle to use our facilities to the fullest, there is the hand of God. There will always be death, destruction, pain and suffering. It is the way of the imperfection of the creative process. But there will always be love, courage, caring, quality and all the higher wonders that make us human. Through these higher qualities, drawn from another plane of reality, God is always with us.

A LOOK AT RELIGION

"Science without religion is lame,
religion without science is blind."

Einstein

Having resolved once and for all the question of evil, I turn to the institution charged with the task of defeating the so called Satanic force, thus saving our immortal soul; namely the organized Church. My background is deep in Roman Catholic belief. Growing up in an Italian American family, the exposure to the Church began at an early age. My particular battleground was Saint Rita's RC Church in the East New York section of Brooklyn, New York - the City of Churches. The love/hate relationship began early in the first few years of elementary school.

To the unknowing, indeed there were nuns; hoards of women, wearing starched black habits from the Batman collection. With rosary beads dangling at their side, they roamed every morning throughout the halls of the schools. All rumors and innuendos concerning their sexuality placed aside, they were well meaning, religious ladies, who taught every subject under the sun to oversized classes of sixty or more incorrigibles. Teach they did, discipline they did, and remarkably, succeed they often did.

In addition to the endless hours of English grammar, and arithmetic recitations, religion was the daily fare. Actually, the local parish church and its parochial school were so interwoven as to make any attempt to distinguish one from the other meaningless. Our Bible was the Baltimore Catechism - the first book opened every morning. The questions and answers contained in those hollowed pages were augmented by frequent visits from a parish priest or, if we were truly fortunate, the pastor himself. "Good morning, Father So and So", the class would shout as the students rose to greet the opening door. Boys bowing, girls in full curtsey – all under the watchful grimace of the lady in black, standing in the corner, clutching her ruler tightly in hand.

But as the strict religious doctrine was being drummed into me, questions arose. The first involved the relationship between my Father and Mortal Sin. Mortal Sin – the severest of transgressions that causes a separation from the heart, love and salvation of God. A black stain on our soul, and if by reason of tragic happenstance, one should die without having the stain removed by the cleansing sacrament of Penance (now called Reconciliation) the unfortunate spirit is destined to spend an eternity damned to the painful fires of hell. The thought of being singed by painful fires should be sufficiently upsetting, but eternity is a mystifying concept. I recall a priest during one Sunday sermon trying to make infinity meaningful. Remove each parcel of sand from every beach on Earth, grain by grain, he instructed. Then take each grain of sand individually on a trip to the moon. Repeat the trip with each grain. When finished, only one second on the clock of eternity will have ticked away. Fire forever – an existence of transporting sand to the Moon - I studied my Catechism all the more intensely.

But how does this relate to my Father? One of the teachings of the church states that the failure to attend Mass is a Mortal Sin. Every Sunday Mass missed, not to mention the attendance required on the Holy Days of Obligation, is yet another mortal sin. Each "stain" individually is capable of damning one to a painful afterlife. I cannot imagine the severity of discomfort the cumulative effect of such failings dictate.

Every Sunday morning my mother would ensure all the children were neatly dressed and at Church. Of course, she accompanied us. I did not realize until much later that in an Italian household, religious matters were traditionally

Frank M. Manfredi

considered women's work. Before leaving for my weekly
religious ritual, I would look in my parent's bedroom, and
see my Father asleep. "Isn't daddy coming?" One of the
children would always ask. My mother would smile, and
tell us "to let him sleep, it was his only day off, and God
would understand."

Week after week, I saw my Father piling on one Mortal
sin after another. Yet, this man was a true example of
perhaps the finest generation brought forth in this Country.
Emigrating from Italy at an early age, my Father was raised
during the Depression, fought in World War II, married
upon returning, and devoted his entire life to his wife and
five children. This man worked six days a week from 6AM
to well after dark, performing the tedious labor of hauling
trash. His fingers cut and scarred. Hands blackened from
the dirt, but how content he was in his house. He loved,
cared, and exuded humor that warmed all he touched.

No, how could God punish this man, for staying in bed
Sunday morning, when his whole life was a testament to
love, caring, work and family? Was all this goodness to be
lost by a mere technical failure? Could God be so cruel?
Or was my mother correct, and the Almighty would
understand? The pages of my Catechism gave no answer.

Nor was my mother spared the pain of the Church's
rigid rulings. One summer, my two brothers and I were
destined for a treat. The YMCA, located around the corner,
from our home, announced the opening of their first
summer camp. A "vacation club" they called it. Trust me,
the daily itinerary pales in contrast to the modern summer
camp. But swimming, a few trips to museums, and the
beach; what more could a youth ask for in the heat of
summer – not to mention the respite my mother would
receive from the difficulty in raising three boys all born
within a few years of each other. Before the camp opened,
however, my mother had a visitor. A local parish priest
arrived and was ushered into our house with a flourish. To

have a priest in the home of an Italian family was ordinarily an honor. Not so on this occasion.

Apparently the parish had learned of my mother's plans for the summer, and the priest carefully instructed my mother that the "C" in YMCA does not stand for Catholic, but Christian. A distinction that would have Christ himself scratching his head in bewilderment. So madam, the priest explained, by sending your children to this camp you will be supporting another religion. This is simply not permissible, and would constitute a sin. I was never sure if the transgression was "mortal" or the more lackluster "venial" variety.

I remember my mother's upset. As a young Italian woman, she drew upon the advice and counsel of other women in our close-knit family. Her mother, sister and aunts were all asked for guidance. Despite the deepest of religious foundations, the feistiness of these ladies was aroused. Suffice it to say, there were three Catholic boys swimming with Protestant lads that summer. Have the heavens ever recovered?

Through it all – the rules and rituals stood my Mother's Mother. Every morning, regardless of the weather, my grandmother somehow made it to daily Mass. If I recall, her daily visit was at 8:10 in the morning unless one of her grandsons was an altar boy at another celebration. There she kneeled, rosary beads in hand, black shroud covering her head, praying – always praying. She attended countless novenas; specific devotions over a period of weeks directed to secure the intercession of a particular saint or in adoration of the Blessed Mother. Our Lady of Perpetual Help, St. Jude and St. Anthony were favorites. Countless candles in adoration were lit. Statutes of Saints touched and kissed; relics cherished. A religious devotion scorned by many today as being ripe with pagan ritual.

But what faith! And who are we to question my grandmother, and those like her. What strength they drew from their beliefs. That faith was the core of her ability to leave one country for another, survive the loss of a child at birth, and lead her family to flourish in a foreign land. Perhaps, I should have lit a few more candles.

Now, my generation has embarked upon a journey seeking true "spirituality". No doubt, this search is fueled in large part by the baby boomers at last tasting their mortality. I wince when I see those who have spent a lifetime seeking material pleasures, now attempting to lead this voyage. Madonna, the epitome of the material girl, quickly comes to mind. But these missions have occurred in the past, and they will happen again. There seems to be a cyclical flow towards this end. The quest, however, is not being led by organized religion. The organized Church, shackled by its past, size, and structure moves slowly, if it moves at all. The role of the Church and its future must be looked at with greater scrutiny.

A LOOK AT RELIGION - (PART II)

"Religion will not regain its old power until it can face change
In the same spirit as does science. Its principles may be eternal,
But the expression of those principles requires continual development."

Alfred North Whitehead

Religion has always been a strong force in civilization. So too, in prison life. Behind the walls, the chapel provides a location, outside of the watchful eyes of the authorities or "hacks" (Horse Ass Carrying Keys) for religious celebrations and as a needed meeting place for inmates. You name the religious following, and it is represented in prison. All recognized sects are there, including a few of questionable validity. Before I left, a few inmates were attempting to secure state clearance for the Church of Witches.

Islam is heavily represented. So too, are the evangelistic and born-again sects of Christianity. Bibles and Korans abound. Religious reference books are used to investigate the most obscure Old Testament verses. One hears, "God Bless You" so often, you would think the prison is in the midst of a sneezing epidemic. It is oxymoronic how, in this environment of daily violence and depravity, the Word of God bears such importance.

Some inmates seem sincere, and occasionally exhibit remarkable positive transformations. Certainly, the devotion is not real for all. The vast majority has found religious activity a means to replace one type of neurotic behavior with another. Still, others seek foolishly to influence the powers in an attempt to secure Parole.

27

Regardless of the numerous reasons for seeking God in jail, the question exists as to why there is such an emphasis on religion while in confinement. The answer lies in the basic concepts contained in the teaching. Forgiveness for their failings (and in many instances these failings are truly monstrous), and the joy of unconditional love are the underpinnings of the religious experience. These are virtues, unfortunately, denied the prisoner by society. Add to total forgiveness and unconditional love, the promise of redemption and the formula is complete.

For a prisoner, these qualities do not exist outside of religious devotion. As remarkable as human love is, it never completely forgives a transgression. Human love preaches forgiveness. And in fact tries valiantly to meet that goal, but human love seems to touch the edge of forgiveness and then backs away. People are scarred by the past. Wounds run deep in our psyche and become part of our very essence. Try as we might; complete, total, unrelenting forgiveness is not within our nature. Somehow, someway, something happens to irritate the scar. The wounds then seep through anew. We deal with it. Build relationships in spite of the hurt, but are never truly forgiven.

If forgiveness and unconditional love is difficult for humans, redemption then for a prisoner is impossible. No matter what heights a felon achieves after his confinement is completed, the individual will always be considered by society as a convict. Often the prisoner wears invisible stripes for many years after the handcuffs are removed. To the inmate who achieves a religious transformation, love, forgiveness and redemption is not sought from the outside world, but is satisfied by religious beliefs.

In my own travels through the prison system, I found myself drawn to my religious roots. At first, attending Mass was an escape from the cell. Slowly, it started to take on a deeper meaning. Ironically, I believe that organized religions contain the framework to lead the quest for spirituality. If only they would grasp the opportunity. There is much that is right with religion.

It is a paradox; at times the very strength of the Church can be its greatest liability. People are the sole purpose of religion. The leaders, be they called priests, ministers, rabbis, imans or head witch, have dedicated their lives to assist their fellow man through the maze of suffering and pain to achieve everlasting salvation. But these efforts are for naught without the congregation. People coming together to worship. The community, all with the same fears, anxieties and hurts, seeks to find the answers. There is no greater altruistic combination.

Even the rituals inherent in organized forms of worship serve an important purpose. Self-discipline is a necessary quality for proper growth. Symbolic rituals can help to foster this habit. Unfortunately, the Church tends to mystify these services to such a degree that the real value namely to strengthen character, and to remember the past is obscured.

As to other failings, all institutions are subject to corruption when run by mortals. History shows that the Catholic Church was not insulated from these defects of human nature. No intelligent Catholic would embrace the precepts that gave rise to the Crusades, the Medieval Popes, or the Inquisition. Nevertheless, the Church has the tools necessary to lead the search for spiritual well being. In order to succeed, however, the focus of the teaching must change. No longer must religion be the source of pain or guilt. Enough suffering permeates our existence.

As I have noted elsewhere in these essays, the "why" of suffering is the greatest of mysteries. To be sure, if any mere mortal were assigned the task of creating a universe, only a fool would devise this current scenario. For whatever the mystical reason, pain and suffering is necessary for our existence. At times I believe that the fleeting moments of joy and happiness are only vacations from the inevitable suffering in our daily life. Sometimes, the very moment of joy contains the seed of future pain. But without pain, conflict and suffering there would be no growth. Suffering is the key.

And the teachings of the Church must recognize the meaning of suffering. Take the belief that Christ died for our sins. What a nonsensical notion. To whom would such an offering be made? Certainly, his Father God Almighty would not require such a sacrifice. Such a vengeful concept belies the goodness and unconditional love of the Creator. Nor would such an offering be made to Satan. The Evil One would not warrant serious consideration from the Son of God.

The death of Jesus, as symbolized by the Cross, shows both the necessity of, and eventual victory over suffering. The paradox is that only through suffering can we grow, only by dying can we live.

The questions I asked as a youth about my Father's religious misdeeds have been answered. My God is not vengeful or punishing. The Force, Energy, Will or Absolute Power that created a Universe so vast and complex, yet so personal and simple is incapable of willfully inflicting pain. My God is one of pure love, unbounded forgiveness, and magnificent creativity. The Church must embrace the suffering of its congregation. Not by providing trite platitudes about the Will of God tossed about to soothe the hurt or answer the unanswerable. It is not the will of the Father that we suffer or hurt. It is simply – the way. The manner in which our species grows and learns in this finite existence.

Teach us to love. Show us the way to bear our pain. Teach us that Christ did not come to protect us from suffering, but to help us in our suffering. If the Church focuses on love, forgiveness, and the truth of human suffering, then it can lead in this search for spirituality.

Incidentally, my father did eventually confess his failings. When I married, he received the Sacrament of Penance. It was well over twenty years since he had been to mass, let alone confession. The local parish priest, a true saint, recognized my Father's plight, and gently led him through the procedure. At the end, the priest smiled, and told my Father to "keep up the good work." That is love and forgiveness in action.

Frank M. Manfredi

THE TOOLS

"Or watch the things you gave your life to broken,
And stoop and build'em up with worn out tools."
"If" Rudyard Kipling

Several years ago, Home Box Office produced a made for television film entitled, "First Time Felon". The plot is simple. Two gang members are imprisoned for selling drugs. Since this was their first exposure to the criminal justice system, they were offered a chance to dramatically reduce their sentence by participating in a military style program designed to instill values and discipline. Many states have enacted similar programs.

For the two hours we watch these street youths. We learn what happened during their period of incarceration and the effect of the program upon their eventual return to society. As you might surmise, in the prison setting this film was mandatory viewing. And as an instructor, I perhaps hold the record of having viewed this film more then anyone.

Despite the simplicity of the plot, the film exists on several interesting levels. A flood threatens the community, and the turning point of the movie occurs when the prisoners were permitted to mingle with the town folk to face this danger. Under the watchful eyes of the prison authorities, the convicts worked with the civilians to control the rising river. Hour after hour the prisoners sweat building sandbagged walls. They worked hard, and followed instructions. Then, the waters rose. The flood level was higher and more ferocious then predicted. Slowly the mountain of sandbags gave way. Our hero desperately tried to pack more sand in a vain attempt to stop the unstoppable. Finally, he was pulled from the wall, cursing through his tears. The flood won and flowed through the

32

town destroying everything in its wake. The prisoners, once so full of pride and purpose, were now despondent. They believed they failed the townspeople, who had given them a chance and a taste of respect.

In a touching moment, a woman from the town brought some food to the men, asking them to come and eat with the others. Although the prisoners were not able to stop the flood, they were able to buy some time, she told them. The people used those few hours to save their furniture, tools, livestock, and other valuables. Thus they were in a position to rebuild. For that they were thankful.

Allegories abound throughout the film, but I was most fascinated with the meaning of the flood. Somehow it captured the essence, not only of this film, but also of our human struggle. These men did every thing right. They worked, prayed, and followed instructions to perfection. Yet, they failed. The flood is the allegory for life. It flows from all directions, sometimes peaceful; often violent with an uncontrollable force that sinks all who challenge its fury. In the face of the randomness of reality, in the face of the imperfection evidenced by a finite existence, there are no guarantees. You can do everything correctly. You can toil from dawn to dusk. Or, study and create every hour of the day. You can have a personality that would charm the gods, and yet you may fail. That is the sad reality of this existence. This is not a pessimistic or depressing view, but reality rearing its head. And too often, that head is ugly indeed.

As the movie aptly points out, we need an instruction book on how to deal with the ebbs and flows of reality. How can we respond to the suffering and uncertainties in life, while enjoying the immense pleasures available? No carpenter would ever consider working on a piece of wood without his bag of tools. They are the craftsman's most valuable asset. Regardless of his knowledge and experience he cannot succeed in the simplest of tasks without the proper tools. That is what we, as humans, also require - a set of life instructions. The tools, if you will, that permit us to face daily uncertainties. The tools become the armor that allows us to take the pounding from the flood that is life, and still have a meaningful, successful, pleasurable existence.

These next few essays discuss these tools. Remember, the importance of these traits is not based upon the writings of self-help gurus, or positive thinking ostrich-like-head-in-the-sand preachers, but advice drawn from my life, a direct result of the failure to consistently apply these tools to the challenges of living. I know that if a person embraces these concepts; no matter what life throws at them, they will be a success. They will earn the respect of those they love. They can look into the mirror every night, and face the only person who matters and smile. Unfortunately, there is no quick fix. These concepts require a great deal of work to develop. Only then can the tools be used instantaneously in life situations. But that is part of the struggle to be what we are.

THE KEY

"While…fear of punishment may restrain us from doing
wrong, it does not make
us wish to do right. Disregarding this simple fact is the
great error into which
parents and educators fall when they rely on these
negative means of correction.
The only effective discipline is self-discipline, motivated by
the inner desire
to act meritoriously in order to do well in one's own eyes,
according to
one's own values…"

Bruno Bettelheim

Now let us leave the metaphysical and deal with the mundane. Everyone wants to be a success. But no one spends any time defining the term. The concept is elusive, because life is constantly changing. One who is viewed as a success today can be eligible for homeless status a few days thereafter. I am reminded of the Supreme Court's musing on the difficulty in defining obscenity. "I can't tell you what it is, but I know it when I see it." Success is very similar. We know when we see success. Whether in business, education, sports or family relationships, success is a state that beams to others from the inside of a person. The problem, however, is determining what traits help achieve that state, so longed for by us.

It is almost humorous. We can go to any store, and purchase the most complex piece of machinery. As soon as we open the box there is the one item we can't wait to tear open, the instruction booklet. Yet, here we are, more complex then any piece of equipment yet conceived, and there are no instructions. Nothing that tells us what steps we must take to achieve happiness. If I had to choose one instruction, one character trait that was essential to ensure success, the answer is simple. The execution, however, is difficult. The ability to deny instant gratification for a purpose is the core ingredient of success.

I was fascinated by the recitation of the marshmallow test in Daniel Goldman's, Emotional Intelligence. Young school children were told that they had a choice, either take one marshmallow now, or wait until the teacher returned from an errand, and get two marshmallows at that time. Very few chose to wait. But those few were watched carefully throughout school. They were the ones with the highest marks and the greatest achievements. During parts of my prison stay, I was fortunate to be an instructor. When I brought up this subject for discussion, I had to make it extremely clear, that the teacher left the room with the marshmallows. The first time I told the tale, I failed to mention that fact. Of course, my students, well versed in thief, petty or otherwise, made it known that the only appropriate choice was to take and eat all the marshmallows while the teacher was out of the room. Once the criminal response was removed we were able to discuss the concept more intelligently. The ability to subdue the desires of the emotions and our appetites, and deny the urge for instant gratification separates the successful from the masses.

To shut off the television, and forego Monday Night Football or a televised Brittany Spears concert for the pain of struggling with a school science project can not be done by many. Saving 10% of income each and every paycheck is a talent known only to the 5% who will have financial independence at the time of retirement. The denial of instant gratification and the self-discipline it engenders is a learned trait. A habit formed, necessary to conquer the momentary and most fleeting of pleasures.

I started my prison term at Sing Sing. Trust me, that jail is misnamed. No one sings there, unless of course they are high on smuggled drugs. Every two weeks we were permitted to go to the commissary, and use the monies we had earned or received from outside the wall to buy necessities, and a few treats. The greatest treasure was a pint of ice cream every two weeks. How we longed for that day. We talked about it, and like children hearing the sound of the ice cream truck of our youth, we rushed to the commissary at our appointed time. Back at our cells, we opened the pint and for a few moments savored the pleasure that those on the outside take for granted. Real ice cream was heavenly. But in a few minutes it was gone. The pleasure did not last. It never does. Soon it is replaced with the reality of life, and that reality is the day-to-day pain and suffering of existence. It may seem silly, but I came to realize that life is a great deal like that pint of ice cream. Oh, it was wonderful to relish that delight. But since it was over so quickly, I knew that it was safer to learn to deal with reality, and understand the daily pains and inevitability of suffering in life.

The ability to deny instant gratification does not work in a vacuum, however. The second part of my definition gives import to the first. The denial must be affixed to a purpose. Not a goal, but a purpose. The difference may seem subtle, but it is vital. I am not a true believer in the benefit of goals. I have seen failures, who have written a daily plan, followed by a five-year goal analysis, with a 10 year plan serving as an umbrella. They have written down their goals, usually on index cards, vocalized them, fine tuned the plan and then failed miserably. In fact, sometimes it seemed they spent more time in planning then they did in doing. Doing is more important then planning. Those who follow the myth of goals, fail to notice another stark reality, namely the ghost of Murphy's Law. Yes, what can go wrong will go wrong, and at the worst possible time. Murphy's findings rival Newton's Laws on Motion for scientific validity.

Countless numbers have felt the edge of Murphy's sword. Good people, hardworking, all following their goals; yet decimated by unforeseen forces. Think of the manufacturers of men's hats, that January 20th in 1961, when John F. Kennedy walked in frigid weather, hat in hand in the inaugural parade ending a trend in fashion that had been in existence for centuries. For many years, engineers and mathematicians made use of a device known as a slide rule. With this tool, all types of complex computations could be conducted with ease. Within a few months in the late 1960's, the calculator emerged, sending these devices to museums, and their manufacturers to bankruptcy. The makers of men's undershirts cringed, when Clark Gable in It Happened One Night removed his shirt to reveal a bare chest. I understand that the effects were devastating, both to the undershirt makers, and to the women who witnessed that scene – time and time again.

The vagaries of life and the reality of Murphy make the use of goals a nebulous tool. But a purpose is different.

A personal experience, I believe, will highlight the difference. When I started my tour of the New York State prison system, despite the non-violent nature of my crime and the length of sentence, I was assigned to maximum security facilities. I survived Sing Sing, Attica, and Green Haven prisons. (Please note that I refuse to use the current politically correct euphuism – correctional facility – to describe jail.) Finally, after repeated attempts my classification came down to medium status, and I was transferred to Fishkill. The worst was supposed to be over. Geographically, I was close to home, and the freedom of a medium was a welcome respite from the lockdowns of the maximum jails.

As in all prisons, the only release is the exercise yard. There prisoners, myself included, would exercise or walk for hours to pass the time. I often would walk alone, not wanting to hear the nonsensical conversations of many of the inmates. One morning, I saw someone who was also transferred from Green Haven. We would nod in silence. One afternoon, I approached him, and asked for permission to walk with him. Behind those walls lies a civilization in and of itself, and special protocols exist. For example, inmates walk in the yard in a counterclockwise direction, and you ask for permission to walk with someone. This man fascinated me. He was quiet, a loner. In the course of our conversations I learned that he had been incarcerated for 20 years for two murders he performed as a contract killer. Because his record was exemplary, his classification was reduced to medium status, and he was permitted to enjoy some of the freedoms of this facility. I noticed that he never went to the store. He never smoked, and did not drink coffee. (The inmates call this doing your "bid" "allstate" – surviving with the minimum items provided by the State).

I questioned him about his austere life style. He stated that he only went to the store once a year. Saving all of the monies earned from his prison labor - a princely sum of $4.50 per week, he would accumulate the monies in his inmate account. When the sum totaled $1,000, he asked for permission to open a Certificate of Deposit. After all that time behind bars, he saved enough to open 3 CD's and was proud to have $3,000 in his possession. Someday he hoped to be released. Since he outlived all the members of his family, he would need some monies to start his life properly.

I went back to my living quarters (In maximum prisons you live in a cell. In mediums you have a cube with a bed and locker area. More freedom, but a locked cell provides greater security for a prisoner, but that is another story). I was amazed at the self-discipline displayed by this man. To forgo even the most minimal of pleasures to secure a benefit far down the road was the epitome of my newly discovered rule.

My conversations with this prisoner took place during the early part of May. My youngest son, Andrew was to have his 10th birthday in September. Moved by this lesson of self-discipline, I established a goal. I would start saving my income and arrange to have a gift of $100 sent to my son on his birthday. After all as a library clerk, I was earning the sum of $7.00 per week, and my sacrifice would not be as great as the other inmate. I stopped smoking Class A cigarettes (the type you can buy in any store), and started to smoke the self-rolling kind. I stopped drinking the expensive instant coffee, and went to the cheaper brand instead. Soon my account started to rise, and I was in a position to make my goal weeks before my son's birthday.

Suddenly Murphy decided to visit. My prison discipline record was pristine. I was never a problem, and I learned to mind my own business. The cops never bothered me because I kept my mouth shut, and represented no threat to them physically. One day, while in my cubicle reading, I looked up to see the officer approaching. He looked troubled and I knew immediately something was wrong. He was almost apologetic as he told me to go downstairs and sign for two Tier 3 tickets alleging violations of the discipline code. It seems that the mother of an inmate wrote to me and asked me to help her son, who was still at Green Haven, with his criminal appeal. While at Green Haven I did assist inmates who were unable to help themselves. But I did not continue the practice when my classification was reduced to medium status. I never saw the letter - Never had it in my possession - Never talked to this woman. And I had no dealings with the inmate after I left the previous prison. Yet, I was accused of corresponding with an inmate, and practicing law without the permission of the prison. Both offenses were serious violations of the code.

I asked for a hearing on the charges. A Mr. Pico was assigned as the hearing official. He was a tiny man, the epitome of a Napoleon complex, with a notorious reputation. He enjoyed the power conferred upon him by the State, and reveled in sending people to the box. I relied upon the facts, the testimony of the women who wrote the letter, the other inmate, the Catholic Chaplins from both prisons. Yet, Mr. Pico decided that although I was innocent of corresponding with the inmate, he considered the letter as a "prelude" to my helping him, and thus I was guilty of the second charge of practicing law without the permission of the prison officials. My sentence was 60 days in the "box", solitary confinement. So on July 3rd I began my sentence. On the 60th day, I was transferred far from the City to a small prison near the St. Lawrence Seaway called Governeur. There I appealed the finding and the administrative office in Albany, New York quickly reversed the holding expunging any reference to the infraction on my record.

My goal was shattered by circumstances far outside my control. My purpose, however, could never be destroyed. My purpose was to show my son, that I loved and cared for him, despite my circumstances. Murphy's Law cannot defeat a purpose. It may delay the fruition, but never defeat the desire. Indeed, goals are important as small road maps to achieve the purpose. But flexibility is important. Take the goal wrap it in unbridled enthusiasm. Embrace it and make it part of your being. Now you have a purpose. Deny instant gratification for that purpose, and you have the key to unlock the door to success.

DEFINITIONS

"Language fails not because thought fails, but because no verbal symbols can do justice to the fullness and richness of thought."

John Dewey

Words are used to portray concepts. A shorthand, if you will, for the ideas they represent. The use of words and language is the best method yet devised to convey what is going on in our heads. Sometimes, however, the words become garbled, the concepts confused and interchangeable. I believe it is important to revisit some terms that are bantered about and examine these concepts as they apply to a successful life. Let us look at the three "self's": self-love, self-image, self-esteem.

We have been told that it is vital in life to love one's self; hence the concept of self-love. We should ooze self-esteem, while always maintaining a proper self-image. But each one of these concepts contains traps and the seeds for failure. Take self-love, for example. In the course of discussing this concept with anyone, I can almost hear the automatic response – "You can't love anyone, unless you love yourself." Bunk, or baloney, which ever you prefer. The ability to love another has nothing to do with loving one self. To the contrary, love is the consummate example of giving, not the self-indulgence contemplated by many who use the concept of self-love. Although every one can repeat the above adage, few can describe with specificity what constitutes "self-love".

Self-love is a component of a healthy psyche. Simply, in every situation, at all times, in all ways, you are important. You may not be correct, but you are important. Recognizing this importance must then be weighed in each particular situation. The other person's wants and needs must be considered as well. Therefore, the idea of self-love is a problem because to focus solely on the importance of self can create problems when dealing with others. Other people have the right to love themselves as well. Of course recognize that you are important, but realize that the other person's position may be valid. And depending upon the situation, your needs should give way to other interests.

Self–image creates its own traps. Unfortunately, our image is created at an early age, and often does not properly reflect how the outside world views us. Far too often our image is wrong. It may be inflated, or understated. It may create an improper picture of our physical characteristics, or intellectual capabilities. The problem is that our mind always fights to protect the image we have of our self. Picture our image as a fine painting encased in a security system. When something goes wrong, our internal security system views the occurrences as an attack on that image and slants the perceptions to protect us. That is one reason why so many really good people do "bad" things. Their views have been instantaneously slanted to protect that picture captured deep in our psyche. This is not offered as an excuse for bad behavior, but merely an example of the evolutionary protection that is part of our survival instinct.

Perhaps an example is warranted. While walking through a crowded store filled with narrow aisles of fine china, ordinary care should be taken. But if I speed through the narrow aisles swinging a briefcase, the result will be inevitable. Hearing the crash of expensive china around me, the immediate instinct is an expletive followed by a remark about my stupidity. Out of the corner of my eye, I see the owner approaching, waiving his hands wildly over his head. Within a nanosecond, my protectors rush to the side of my self-image. I am not clumsy; I am graceful, elegant, and I could not be responsible for this act. By the time the owner reaches me excuses for the accident flow from my lips – the aisles were too narrow – the china was

43

piled negligently – thank God I wasn't injured – I should sue etc. In order to protect my sacrosanct self-image, the mind instantly skewed my perceptions creating excuses and other explanations for the occurrences.

The last of the troublesome "self's" is that of self esteem. This one is tricky. Obviously, it is generally accepted that a healthy self-esteem is important for building a successful life. I define self-esteem, as that which makes us "feel" good about ourselves. The problem is the part of the definition that "feels". That which makes us feel good is not often what is best for us. For example, if I were to go out with $500 in my pocket, I tend to feel more successful. If I were going to a club to meet a lady, I would feel more "sexy" with that money in my pocket then if I only had a twenty dollar bill. Self-esteem tends to rise or fall because of external factors. And that is dangerous. When we follow that which feels good, we fail to recognize the concepts that are truly important.

Remember the old "chicken or the egg" controversy. What came first? The same question applies to self-esteem. What comes first the internalized feeling of a healthy self esteem or is that feeling of self esteem derived as response to exterior sources? I am the same person whether I have $500 or $5 in my pocket. But once I have that money something changes inside, and I feel better about myself, more successful. Is it the action of the mind or the body that causes this feeling of success? At times it seems the thought comes first, and the body follows. On other occasions, the mind seems to follow the body.

Anyone who physically exercises on a regular basis knows this problem. You awake in the morning not wanting to do even the easiest of stretches. Then once the first push up is completed, more easily follow. The objections of the mind seem to dissipate with the action of the body. Soon the mind is telling the body to go for just one more push up. The popular saying, "fake it till you

44

make it" is just such an example of the mind following the actions of the body.

Self-love is over rated; self-image is by nature often skewed. Self-esteem relies upon external triggers to make us feel good. Each of these three types of "self" can cause the validation of our existence, who we are, to depend upon external factors.

The answer is another form of "self" - that of self worth. Of all the values that exist, I believe the most important are integrity and quality. I have devoted one specific essay to these concepts. If a person is rebuilt from the inside to be a person of integrity living a life of quality, then there is self-worth. That self worth comes from the deepest parts of our being. There is no need to love ourselves, since our love is derived from our worth. There is no need to create a healthy self image, because our image is irrelevant if met with a deep sense of worth, and finally it is not necessary to "feel" good about ourselves because our self worth gives us the tools to survive in those times, too numerous to mention, when things will not go well. The only "self" that matters is the worth of a person. And worth is a direct result of integrity and quality.

While I am at it, let me throw in a few other definitions that I feel are important. Respect is a concept that is tossed about, especially by the young. Everyone thirsts for respect. I suggest the use of this term in popular parlance is all wrong. I have no duty to respect anyone. Respect is earned by one person from another. I have a duty to love everyone, and by love I mean not to harm any other individual. I have a duty to exhibit tolerance, and by tolerance I mean giving other persons space to be the best individuals they can be. But no duty to respect exists.

When I respect someone, I am conferring upon that person, a piece of myself. My approval as to what that person is about. When I confer that acceptance, I am giving something important, a part of me, and that part should only be conferred after it is earned. In my own circumstances, I have no right to be respected. I have hurt people, and caused untold hardship. Perhaps, I am loved by close family, but not respected. That respect must be earned. Someday perhaps, from those around me, acceptance may come my way. But as I have tried to say that is no longer important. By working to develop self worth, my validation comes from within, and not from others.

Personality and character are two other words often used interchangeably. They are not the same. Character is formed at the deepest levels of our being. It is a compilation of our intellect, emotions, and value structure. It is who we are. Or as the youth say – what we are about. Personality, on the other hand, is the mechanism used to reveal our character to others. Hitler had a remarkable, dynamic, personality. His character, however, was suspect to say the least. Curiously, our personality develops in part to hide a portion of our character we do not want others to see. Part of the reason for this deception results from our failure to delve deeply to determine precisely who we are: and to delve we must.

WHAT IS YOUR IQ LEVEL?

*"Necessity may well be called the Mother of Invention
but Calamity is the Test of Integrity"*
Samuel Richardson

*"People of Quality know everything without
Ever having learned anything."*
Moliere

Values, values, values. Family values, religious values, personal values, sexual values, national values, on and on preach the spokespeople of our time. Cajoling, castigating and commiserating about the lack of values in our society, and specifically lamenting over the lack of values in our youth. I find it amusing, however, that those same people who preach the value ethic, are really saying that it is their values that they want adopted. Often the same individuals, who argue against abortion citing the value of life, have no difficulty in closing their eyes to a lethal injection that kills someone on death row.

Indeed, there are values that form the core of society; the prohibition against murder is an example. But as we move away from the basics, the area gets very murky. Values are personal, and should not be dictated by forces outside ourselves. In any event, the entire question really turns on two qualities that must serve as the basis for our character formation, and hence our value structure.

A few months ago, I was having an argument with a salesman. This proud representative of an electrical supply house was trying to explain why a promised shipment was more then 2 weeks late. I was demanding to know why he was unable to return my phone calls as to the status of the order. In the course of this somewhat loud discussion, I

47

asked him what was the IQ level of his company. He turned and gave me a blank stare and started explaining that all the people at his company were quite intelligent. "No," I answered, "Not Intelligence Quotient, but IQ, IQ." "What is the level of Integrity and Quality in your company?" I would rather deal with a moron who displayed integrity and a high level of quality then with all the certified geniuses in the world.

When these words were blurted out in anger, I realized that these two qualities, or traits, are a vital factor in character development. Integrity and Quality form the base of a proper value ethic. Intellect and education are irrelevant when it comes to character and values. Trust me; I am evidence of that fact. The higher your integrity - quality level, the stronger your character formation becomes, and the more sincere your value ethic. Integrity and quality are two simple words. But when you take the time to think about the concepts that these words represent, you stumble into areas that have troubled the greatest philosophers throughout time. Let us delve into these concepts, and see how these qualities are applied in daily life.

What is integrity? What does it mean when you look at someone and know that he or she is person of integrity? What qualities comprise this air? Our first instinct is to make integrity synonymous with honesty, or truthfulness. No doubt, honesty is an important part of integrity. Yet, there is more. Integrity is derived from an old Latin word meaning "whole". What is this wholeness? First, look at honesty. Coming from a background where the word lawyer and liar were often used interchangeably, I am quite familiar with the term. Is every untruth uttered a lie? No. Only, a person, who speaks words known to be untrue, lies. This definition has two independent elements. First, the words must not reflect truth, and secondly, the speaker must know that they are false. It is possible to be wrong, or to make a mistake, and not lie. The scienter element, the knowledge that what is spoken is false, is missing; thus, no lie.

Silence can also be construed, at times, to be a lie. This is a little more complex, then the spoken falsehood, but I believe that when your failure to speak will make someone do something against their interests, you have committed a lie of omission. For example, the roof in your house leaks, but the buyer does not ask, and you do not tell. Have you lied? - In a way. Your silence caused another to pay more than the house may have been worth. For our purposes, however, we can avoid controversy and deal with the run of the mill spoken lie.

It makes no difference why a falsehood is told. We always create a rationale for the lie. Perhaps, the speaker is acting under a sincere, albeit misguided, desire to protect the recipient of the lie. Or, the liar may be attempting to realize some concrete gain from the falsehood. At all times, the liar receives some benefit, whether physical or psychological. With few exceptions, such as to save a life, that benefit does not forgive the utterance of an untruth with knowledge of the falsity of the statement. Simply stated, honesty is using your word to state what is real.

Integrity, however, is more. Yes, honesty is an essential element, but it is combined with the ancient Greek notion of honor. Defining honor is difficult, but honesty coupled with honor creates the wholeness satisfying the Latin root of integrity. While honesty is using your word to state what is real, integrity can be defined as making real that which is your word. An example is in order.

In prison, there is no greater asset then a pack of cigarettes. "Smokes" are money behind the wall. It stands to reason, therefore, that a carton of cigarettes, or "crate" in the prison vernacular, is a veritable fortune. One day, while walking in the yard, a fellow inmate approaches with a worried look on his face. Whether because of a gambling or drug obligation (both situations exist in great numbers in prison) he is in debt. Prison debt cannot be absolved by bankruptcy. It must be properly addressed, because the collection techniques involve scarring of facial tissue, or worse a trip to the hospital with a shank implanted in your chest. The situation then is serious. Since I know the prisoner, and recognize the seriousness of the situation, I agree to help. In our conversation, I explain that I am expecting a visit, and will be getting several cartons of smokes on Sunday. Out of friendship, I agree to loan him the carton. We arrange to meet in the prison yard on Tuesday to deliver the smokes before he has to pay his creditor.

All seems well, too well in fact. As Murphy's Law mandates, it snows heavily on Saturday, and my visit cancels. No visit, no package – no cigarettes! Being a person motivated by honesty, I search out the other inmate and inform him of the reality. It is now Monday, and he has less then 24 hours to come up with the payment or face the consequences. He nods in solemn understanding. Thanking me for trying to help. After all, it is his problem, not mine. He walks away worried and frightened. What happened in this situation? Was I not the picture of honesty? Was not my desire to help a fellow human motivated by sincere concern? And when the failure to produce the cigarettes was caused by factors clearly outside of my control did I not act promptly and openly to inform this man of the problem? Was not every word spoken truthful – real? Absolutely! I acted with integrity – right? Not quite.

In this example, my honesty factor was exemplary, but was the honor component of the integrity definition satisfied? Did I make my word reality? True, the failure to keep the commitment was due to factors outside of my control. I assure you the prison guards would not permit a trip to the local 7-11 to purchase a carton of cigarettes. Recognizing the seriousness of the situation, there was more that could have been done to address the honor concept of integrity and bring the reality closer to my word. Perhaps, I could agree to meet with the creditors and explain the situation. Or, I could have delved into my own stock and produced a few packs to buy some time. Even more, I could have used my own credit rating to borrow a carton to meet the commitment that came from my own lips. Each one of these steps has nothing to do with being honest, but they do have a direct relationship to one's honor. Taken together they serve to increase integrity.

This must be emphasized. With a few exceptions, I am duty bound to be honest – to use my word to reveal what is real. I am under no duty to commit to take an action, and thereby invoke the honor component. In the prison yard example, I could easily have said no to the other person. Once I choose to act, however, I cannot be deemed to be a person of integrity unless both factors, honesty and honor, are addressed. Perhaps you recall the following scene. In the George Lucas film The Empire Strikes Back, Luke Skywalker crashed his X-Wing fighter into a swamp. Struggling to master the power of the Force, Luke has sought the instruction of the Jedi Master, Yoda. Luke is asked by Yoda to use the Force to lift the waterlogged craft from the swamp. Luke squints, and with a great deal of pain succeeds in lifting the object a few feet from the murk of the swamp. Growing tired, the Jedi wannabe loses concentration, and the fighter falls back to the swamp. I tried Master Yoda, cries Luke. The wise impish Jedi Master then states a phrase that should be basis of any attempt to be a person of integrity. "There is no try", says Yoda. "A Jedi either does or does not."

To do or do not is the essence of the honor component of the integrity definition. If the word is spoken, the commitment made, then the closer you can honestly meet the obligation the greater your integrity. In most circumstances the ability to say no quickly, honestly and with sincerity will suffice. There are times, however, that the "no" or worse yet silence is not the proper response to a situation. Responsibility is also a characteristic of honor, and hence integrity. I define responsibility as a person doing what he knows he should do. Again, this is a two-part definition. The first part involves action. A person must act. In these instances the "no" or silence is wrong. The second part of the definition sometimes causes trouble; the person must know what has to be done. Let us look at another example. A father has a "responsibility" to support his children. No one could disagree with that statement. But if a Father decides to tell the Court that he no longer desires to pay support for his children, he certainly is honest and sincere. But the "no" in this instance is inappropriate. He has failed in his responsibility; the honor part of the definition is lacking, and no amount of honesty will create integrity for that father.

Integrity then is a combination of honesty and honor. When a person acts with integrity, his footing is firm, because the underlying character is strong, and the values that form the basis of integrity, honesty and honor, serve as armor in facing the challenges of life. But what of the second part of the IQ level – that of quality?

I wish this were as easy as integrity. Words and concepts like these make me realize that there must be a God. The word seems simple, but the concept of quality has given rise to an entire division of philosophy. Suppose I gaze at a Stradivarius violin. Most would agree that that object is the epitome of a quality musical instrument. But where is the quality. Does it lie in the object or in the beholder? If it is in the violin itself then the quality should be evident to everyone. That definition means that the concept of quality is objective, existing in reality outside the viewer. If on the other hand, it is the opinion of the viewer that the violin has quality, then the concept is relative, and the notion of quality depends on the perspective of the viewer. But if quality is relative, then nothing can inherently be a quality item - and on and on. What a problem this seven-letter word creates. Yet we seem to know innately when something or someone is quality. It is as though this concept of quality comes from outside the mind, from a higher self or divine creativeness. Thankfully, for our purposes it is not necessary to resolve this philosophical debate.

But one thing is certain. There is a direct relationship between caring and quality. The more someone cares the greater the quality produced. The craftsman who toils at his creative best will undoubtedly produce a product with more quality then someone who takes all the shortcuts. Caring is the key. When people care about what they do, quality results. Further, the more they care, the greater the quality. I believe caring is a divine trait. It invokes feelings of love, concern and creativeness. This ability to care is not limited to the craftsman. The janitor who cares about his work will produce a cleaner environment – greater quality. The computer program designer, for example, who may never meet the end user, by approaching his design with innovative care, creates quality. The salesman who truly cares about his customers creates quality. The corporation that cares about its employees, customers and investors becomes a quality force.

The salesman, I mentioned at the inception of this essay, lacked the caring quality. Of course, it was possible for the shipment to be delayed. But did he truly care? Did he attempt to see if any other resolution of the problem could be effectuated? Did he aggressively work with me to show the depth of his concern?

Nor is caring confined to the business or work environment. To be people of quality, caring must permeate our personal life as well, seeping into all phases of our endeavors. The more caring one is the greater the quality of a love relationship. Friendships, as well, become deeper more meaningful when the care level increases. Even our spiritual understanding deepens when we approach the mysteries of the unknown with caring, because as I mentioned, the ability to care is almost divine. It combines aspects of love and creativity. It produces a quality existence.

So you can keep your discussions of values. Personally, I will work on increasing my own integrity/ quality level, and will gladly deal with anyone who evidences this type of a high IQ.

THE DECISION MAKING QUANDRY

"Two roads diverged in a wood, and I - -
I took the one less traveled by,
And that has made all the difference."
"The Road Not Taken," Robert Frost

Free will is great. The ability as thinking, rational animals to do what we want is perhaps the greatest benefit of the evolutionary leap that brought Homo sapiens to the forefront of the animal empire. As a result of this power, we make countless decisions every day. Most choices are simple, and we act with no noticeable consequence. Many decisions, however, are difficult, and we are forced to use the full range of our talents to choose a particular course of action. Often we are frozen unable to choose any path between two or more courses. We procrastinate and do nothing. Sometimes we act, and then realize that the course chosen is wrong, the consequences dire. What then is the proper way to make a decision?

I know I am going to get into trouble with this chapter. I can state with some certainty that almost all the decisions I made in my life turned out to be wrong. So if my premise is correct, that failure creates knowledge, then I must be wise indeed. Clearly, this is a case of my asking you to do as I say, not as I have done.

The first problem is dealing with the concept of reality. In my younger days, I was convinced that all reality was relative. Perspective was the most important factor. Therefore, reality only exists, as the viewer perceived it. This theory permits different realities to exist. For example, a Japanese sailor on a destroyer, during WW II, from his perspective was performing a vital needed, service as his ship bombed an American vessel a few hundred yards away.

55

On the American ship, the young man loading ammunition was equally convinced, based upon his perspective, that his efforts were mandated by a higher good. Therefore, the reality of the situation depends on whose perspective we chose to view.

Even a micro universe, that realm known as quantum mechanics, gives credence to the concept that reality exists only from the point of view of the viewer. It is part of the theory of quantum physics that the mere act of viewing a phenomenon has the potential of changing the reaction. Thus the underlying reality is uncertain. While in a miniscule universe the actions of a single photon may be affected by the act of viewing, physicists recognize the existence of vast probabilities, and reconcile the perspective difference by limiting the uncertainty to the quanta level.

Unfortunately, the relative view of reality in our plane of existence is wrong. Reality exists separate from the viewer. It exists even if there is no one to perceive it. Remember the old question, "If a tree falls in a forest and there is no one there to hear it, does it make a sound? We know that sound is created by the vibration of our eardrums when waves strike the tissues contained in the ear. So the reality is that there would be no sound unless there was someone to receive it. But the falling tree will create the waves containing the information that can be turned into sound even if no humans existed on the earth. Thus an integral part of sound, the formation of waves, exists without anyone being there.

The failure to realize that reality exists, outside of our perception, is the root cause of many wrong decisions. Yet, it is also a fact that everyone perceives reality differently. This difference in perspective is the result of numerous factors. Differences in education, sociological background, and religious beliefs are but a few of the prejudices that cause variances in people's perception. Add to these items individual quirks such as one's self image or personality, and the divergence between perception and reality increases. When we act solely on our perception of what is real, we get into trouble. The closer our perception mirrors the outside existence of reality the more valid is our decision making process. It may be impossible to walk the reality line all the time. Our perceptions do get in the way. But in making decisions, the first step is to appraise the situation not from our perspective, but from outside ourselves to see the flow of reality. Attempt to freeze your perceptions, and focus on the real by standing outside of yourself to view the situation as it exists without the cloud of our wants or desires.

We must realize that our ability to perceive is limited. Our senses and the level of our empirical knowledge hamper perception. If, for example, I made a decision based upon my perception that the sun circled the earth, I would be wrong. Yet, countless millions in history perceived just that example as reality. Often the example of the error is not that easy.

When I first went astray, I acted solely from perception, not from reality. When I misused someone else's money for the first time, I can still hear my mind bring forth all the noble excuses covering my wrong. "It would only be for a few days." "It is for a good cause, since I am using it to help a client in an immediate crisis." "I can always replace it since I have that next case coming in." etc. etc. I failed to realize that reality has certain rules. The law of cause and effect, the deadening of one's conscience, the quick descent into hell from violating one's principles are just a few of the harsh rules of reality.

The misuse of funds was objectively wrong. No amount of subjective perspective rationalization could change that immutable law. Unfortunately, only bad consequences flow from breaking the laws of reality. And they are all losses – loss of love, loss of respect, the loss of freedom. Not to mention the simple inability to look in the

57

mirror and see your eyes staring back at you. Having suffered all of the foregoing, it is my prayer that unnecessary suffering be avoided by anyone reading these essays.

Back to the decision making process; once you move your perception close to the reality flow, move on. Secure information. Rational, cold hard facts should be a part of any decision. In this era information abounds. But information is not knowledge, and certainly it is not wisdom. It is only a one facet of the process. Further, the wealth of information creates other problems. There comes a point when you must stop. When conducting research for a legal brief or term paper, the critical moment is knowing when you have enough material. Stop and digest the information. Weigh the benefits of each course. Analyze the consequences of each potential action in the face of outside reality. Are there responses that others can take to your actions? Have you thought them through? Have you looked Mr. Murphy and his laws in the face and tried to see what can go wrong? In short, try to use all the rational ability that our distinct form of animal has developed over the countless years. Then turn to your emotions.

Despite our penchant for rational thinking, all of our decisions are made, in some manner, with our heart, our emotions. Our rational mind follows providing rational reasons for the action. The emotions and feelings process information faster then our rational mind. It is important, therefore, that rational thought provide some check on the tug of the emotion. Let us look at a specific example of the process. You and your spouse are expecting a new addition to the family. Together you have decided that it is time to share in the American Dream and buy a house. You have analyzed rationally your finances. You know the amount of the down payment you have available. You have rationally projected your income over the next few years, and have a handle on the expenses that the new expected infant will require. Both of you have settled on a price range that can be reasonably afforded. Proudly, you praise your rational ability. Then you go shopping.

Armed with classified sections and real estate broker in hand, what happens? You can't find anything within the price range you agreed upon. After several weeks of looking at homes, depression creeps in to your conversation. "Are these sellers crazy?" you lament. Slowly you start looking at homes just a little outside your price range. Now they are talking. These houses have that extra room you are looking for. You start looking for additional income. You think about that other deal you are working on. A few weeks ago it had no future, but now looking at these larger homes your mind has already cashed the check. Your mind has started to waiver from the flow of reality, into the perception range. If the process increases, you will soon be computing anticipated inheritances from your parent's insurance policies as you ponder the mortgage and real estate taxes on the mansion that you now feel you deserve.

But there comes a time in the decision on a new house, when you get back to a little closer view of realty, and then almost mystically, you walk into a house, and there is a feeling. You know that you and your family belong there. Emotion takes over. You feel it in your "gut" that this house will be your home. And the final decision is made.

So in making a decision you must recognize reality, secure information, and make use of your rational facilities. Permit your emotion to take over. Feel the right course, and then have that feeling checked by your rational thought. For emotion alone can take you too far a field. When all else fails remember that a bad decision is generally better then no decision at all. Inaction is such a waste of human existence.

Still at a loss. Then take the road less traveled. For some reason, the course of action that contains the most work, the greatest challenge, the largest potential for self-discipline, the risk of failure and suffering, is the right path. Growth comes from challenge and conflict. As I have said elsewhere, it is our way.

THE MORE THINGS CHANGE THE MORE THEY STAY THE SAME

If one person in battle conquerors a thousand men a thousand times,
And another conquers himself,
The second man is the greatest of conquerors
Buddha

The title to this essay is an old cliché. Although these sayings are trite, they have lasted over time, because they contain elements of truth. I recall someone who once editorialized why marriage, as an institution, is doomed to failure. The instant a woman marries she is convinced that she will succeed in changing her husband, and at the very same moment, her husband is convinced that his beautiful bride will never change. Both are wrong, and conflict naturally ensues. But change is a reality, is it not? All things change, argue the pundits. Every day we learn that science cures diseases, yet new illnesses race to take their place. Countries rise and fall today, just as they did in antiquity. We lust, steal, and brutalize one another today, just as in times past. Undoubtedly, we possess more knowledge at this point of our existence then at any time in history, but in reality has anything changed. More importantly, can people really change who they are? Can we change our nature?

Because of my experience, these questions carry special import. Is it possible to truly change what we are, or are we destined to merely cope with the debilitating effects of character flaws and personality failings? I went to prison, not once, but twice. My flaws, so evident to others, were buried under my constant denial, and glib retorts. My first imprisonment was relatively mild. After leaving the county jail, I was transferred to the State facility designed for

61

distribution of inmates throughout the state. Since it was my first offense, and I was a non-violent criminal, I was assigned to a minimum facility for a few months, before granted work release. The penal philosophy was that I had suffered enough, and surely no reasonably intelligent person would return to jail after having a taste of the system.

I will never forget a family dinner a few months after my return. Present among the family was my brother, Arthur. Now AJ, as he is called, will never be mistaken for one of the deepest, compassionate thinkers placed on this earth. He is blessed, however, with an uncannily honest, if not black and white, approach to reality. In the course of the conversation that day, my brother commented that the family was glad that I was home, but that I had not changed.

How those words stung. Slowly, I felt the anger build inside of me. How could he say that? Had I not lost my license to practice law? Didn't he know how embarrassed I was? Didn't he realize that I knew the pain I caused my wife, my children, my mother and father? Of course, I learned my lesson. Of course, I had changed. Approximately 18 months after his observation, I was again in jail, and the State was about to ensure that any leniency previously shown would completely be withheld.

He was right; I did not change. As I entered the cell that first night in jail, and the doors locked behind me, through my tears I thought about that conversation, and was in a daze as to how I permitted this to happen again. Why didn't I change after that first period of confinement? Upon reflection perhaps, the more basic question is whether it is possible to change?

The recipe that made each of us unique individuals is a combination of various random factors. At one time, controversy raged as to whether we were products of nature or nurture. Such fights are silly. Obviously both factors affect our existence. At our core, we are physiologically constructed with DNA codes. These instructions are based upon generations of genetic construction and hereditary traits. We cannot deny that this data creates proclivity in some of us to certain personality disorders. A proclivity, however, is not a certainty. At the same time, we are infused with the instincts, and evolutionary emotions needed by our animal ancestors for their survival. Add to this mix, the influence of our parents and environment in the formative years. Influences, which may appear benign, yet have the effect of sharpening the edge of certain traits over others. This combination of factors is a prescription for disaster.

Then we are thrown out in to the world to deal with other individuals with their own mix of tangled nature and nurture imprints. At times, it is difficult to see how we as a species have progressed this far without destruction. We have to realize that as Homo sapiens, our essence is contained at the deepest of levels. To say that we are complex is to define understatement. Personally, I despise simple answers to complex problems. And from my own experience, I can attest that personal change ranks as the most complex of problems. To state, as many do, "that anyone can change but they have to want to" is untrue. To state as well, "that if you love me (or us) you would change" is also false. The current craze of advice that we have choices, and we choose our action belies the complexities and the depth of our essence.

I recall vividly one night listening to a radio show hosted by a renowned psychobabble personality. A Walkman radio is one of the few comforts permitted in maximum-security prisons. A young girl called in obvious distress. She had just visited her mother in jail for drug possession. Her problem was whether or not she should tell her mother how hurt she felt about her mother's confinement. Quickly, the radio expert agreed that the young girl should share her feelings with her mother, advice that I concur with. Our rationale, however, is substantially different. Tell your mother; because if she knows how much she has hurt you she will stop using drugs was the advice. Having three children myself, one of tender years when the second confinement started, I was very attuned to the hurt caused my children by my additive, compulsive, and irresponsible behavior.

Through my tears, I felt my anger rising. Didn't this so-called expert realize that the women knew the hurt caused her child? She knew and still could not stop! To be sure, this type of discussion can be instrumental in starting change. But true change cannot be generated from the outside. No amount of love for another. No threat of loss of fortune or freedom. No rational understanding of the cause of the problem is sufficient to cause change. All external motivations, no matter how powerful, wane with each passing day as the depth of compulsiveness or addiction seep to the forefront.

We all know the story of Robert Louis Stevenson's, Strange Case of Dr. Jekyll and Mr. Hyde. By drinking a mysterious concoction, the knowledgeable, personable Dr. Jekyll turns into his dark side, releasing the evil Mr. Hyde. There is one part of the story that, I believe, is quite telling. At one point in his transformation, the Doctor turns into the Hyde character, without drinking the serum. It occurred at a juncture in the story when the Doctor swore off the potion, and was quite successful in overcoming his dark desire. But the Hyde character seeped through from its depth. Why? Because it was part of the good doctor's essence. As our darkness is part of our essence.

Why then is it so difficult to change? Simply, there are many things that we cannot change. Much of our character and nature is created at levels too deep to reach. Perhaps years of psychoanalysis can reveal to us the causes of our behavior, but I question its ability to effectuate real change. The knowing of "why" does not mandate change. Often we are left to cope with our defects. Coping mechanisms are important when the trait lies at the deepest levels. Addictive, compulsive, irresponsible, criminal, or negative behavior, however, must be checked.

We are fortunate. As humans we are the only animals capable of attempting real change. It is difficult. What we normally see as changes of behavior is a person replacing one form of compulsion with another. Often that is fine. For example, an alcoholic can replace his addiction with the compulsiveness of the AA program. Occasionally, religious fervor is the tonic to change one's demeanor. But is the change real?

Here is the problem. Our brain is split. We have our rational side. Intellectually, rationally, we know that repeated abuse of alcohol, for example, creates problems in our lives. The promises we make to others and ourselves are short lived. The use of will to avoid alcohol, a response of the rational mind, will succeed for a while. But just as in the case of Dr. Jekyll, the dark side can come forth even without the use of the potion. The causes of the irrational behavior do not come from the thinking mind, they come from the unconscious, that part of our existence that recalls all of our experiences and triggers our animal instincts towards preservation. These deep responses may trigger physiological proclivities contained in our DNA borne from generations past. Trust me; no one with a properly functioning rational mind would welcome the loneliness of prison. Crimes can be premeditated, but the motivation for these acts, power, pleasure, hatred, anger, etc., are derived from our unconscious existence.

And the situation gets worse. The unconscious part of our being responds virtually immediately to impulses or threats whether real or imagined. The mere perception triggers the workings of the unconscious and our emotional responses. The reason is quite simple. Our animal brain is older then the frontal lobes that house rational thought. Our deepest instincts are embedded in our animal responses.

65

After the animalistic responses are sent into motion, an impulse is sent to the frontal lobes to analyze the situation. While the call to the rational brain is sent quicker then we can compute, it is nevertheless later then the instructions sent to the animal part of our brain. Often, that interval, no matter how brief, makes the rational brain too late to slow down the emotions and bad behavior results. That is the reason I believe the current wave of choice therapy is lacking. It is too simple. And we are not simple creatures. Choice is a function of rationality. In order to choose wisely, the rational brain must have the time. But the very nature of the human beast does not afford that luxury, since the forces that exist in our deepest regions are already instantaneously at work.

A brake is needed. Something to slow our behavior until the rational brain has the time to analyze the situation and act. Sometimes nature causes such a breaking. Age, for example, often dulls ones emotions and proclivities towards violence. Raising hands in anger is easier for a young man then an older one. Although I do recall my grandfather, while in his sixties, bat in hand, chasing a car owner who cursed him. Please understand that my thoughts on the difficulty of change are not intended to excuse in any way improper or bad behavior. To the contrary, we have a responsibility to ourselves and others not to cause harm. It is because of this responsibility that change is necessary. The brake must be found.

Values are the brake. There are certain qualities that seem to combine the rational and unconscious mind. Integrity, quality, courage, hope, love, peace, tolerance are examples of traits that come from both parts of the brain, but are created on a different level. Some have called this realm a higher self - others use the term the spirit. But it seems clear to me that a properly functioning human existence requires both the rational and unconscious. They must work together to bring to the forefront the best of humanity. The higher qualities bridge both brain functions forming a synergy where the whole of the brain function is far greater than the components working alone.

An example is in order. Assume a person who has had a history of deceit and lies. That same person has adopted the virtue of integrity, of which honesty is a component. Each day the virtue becomes more ingrained. Suddenly, in the course of a discussion, the person feels physiologically attacked. The tugging; the urge to lie, and thus secure an immediate benefit rises to the forefront. The lie is almost to the tip of his tongue. Relief from the attack is only an instant away. But the person has worked hard to become an individual of integrity. That portion of the virtue of integrity that is housed in the higher self breaks the automatic response. The rational brain takes over, the reason for lying is dismissed, and although the person may stutter for a moment the lie does not come. In time, the process becomes easier. When traits such as integrity or quality are adopted a transformation is possible. Values provide that brief break that permits rationality to overcome instinctive responses, and true choice becomes possible.

Change lies in the ability to adopt meaningful values. In case, anyone was wondering, I am partial to Les Miserables. Victor Hugo's creation of Jean Valjean is an amazing example of psychological insight. After Valjean's incarceration, he steals from a Bishop. But when caught the Bishop forgives and saves Valjean from further police involvement. Because of this external experience, Valjean undergoes deep introspection, and changes his life. Values help in his endeavor. Although often tested, Valjean becomes a man of integrity. He loves and cares.

The author comments that the change is not a mere "transformation, but a transfiguration". True change requires just such a transfiguration of our existence. And the adoption of values is the key. The task is not easy.

Often we stumble. But the challenge is greater then the imprisonment we face from our dark sides.

THE DIVINE QUALITIES

"In the depths of winter I finally learned
there was in me an invincible summer."

Albert Camus

In July 1925, during a sweltering summer in Dayton, Tennessee, two legal giants fought an epic battle. Clarence Darrow and William Jennings Bryan, clashed in the famous Scopes "monkey" trial. More than the right to teach evolution was on trial. The ultimate question of that Court proceeding was really "What, as humans, are we?" Bryan fought hard to enforce the dictates of Genesis, while Darrow battled to vindicate the scientific theory of natural selection. That courtroom drama was fictionalized by Jerome Lawrence and Robert E. Lee in the play entitled Inherit the Wind. In the climatic scene, Bryan, called Matthew Harrison Brady in the play, was on the stand testifying as an expert on the Biblical account of creation. Under withering cross examination by Darrow, renamed Henry Drummond, Brady started to crack. The following exchange was crucial:

<u>Brady:</u> We must not abandon faith! Faith is the important thing.
<u>Drummond:</u>Then why did God plague us with the power to think? Mr. Brady, why do you deny the one faculty which lifts man above all other creatures on earth: the power of his brain to reason. What other merit have we? The elephant is larger, the horse is stronger and swifter, the butterfly more beautiful, the mosquito more prolific, even the simple sponge is more durable! Or does a sponge think!
<u>Brady:</u> I don't know. I'm a man, not a sponge.
<u>Drummond:</u>Do you think a sponge thinks?
<u>Brady:</u> If the Lord wishes a sponge to think, it thinks.

Drummond:Does a man have the same privilege that a sponge does?
Brady: Of course.
Drummond:This man wishes to be accorded the same privilege as a sponge! He wishes to think.

By dramatic device, Drummond was able to ridicule the strict interpretation of Genesis' account of creation that is, remarkably, still held sacred by many today. Far be it from me to be critical of Mr. Darrow, but his championing of the rational, thinking man as the height of human existence sells our species far too short. No one questions the advancements brought to our civilization by the scientific method. The ability to test and prove hypotheses has brought us great technological progress. Yet, we are so much more.

As I have mentioned previously, our brain has evolved in different stages. On one side are our animal instincts, with their resultant emotions and fears. Far more ingrained then our ability to rationally think, these instincts contain awesome power. Obviously though, we are more then the animal response of fight or flight. On the other side, we find the development of our frontal lobes and the ability to be rational. Certainly, we are not limited to the dull computer functions of rational calculation and cold planning. Life is a battle between these two evolutionary forces. But we have tools that appear to soothe the cutting edge between these two diametrically opposed traits.

There are abilities that do not fit neatly within either side of the brain. As conscious beings, we have access to certain qualities that transcend the gift of reason, and dwarf our animal instincts. These qualities, I label as divine. Not necessarily because they come from a divine entity, although they could; but these traits appear to be drawn from some higher plane, a higher self. These divine qualities, when coupled with rational thought and our emotions, constitute total humanness.

These virtues are easy to list but, unfortunately, difficult to define. In a prior essay, I discussed at some length the ambiguity of the virtue of "quality", and the caring that it engenders. Caring and the production of quality in all aspects of our existence is an essential element of a meaningful, "divine" life. At times, it can be logical to be caring. It can be emotionally satisfying to be caring, and perhaps to care is rooted in some deep evolutionary instinct. But to care and create quality seems to transcend the purpose of our rational or instinctive nature. That is one of the reasons for the philosophical debate over whether quality is objective or subjective in nature. Take caring to the extreme level, and we discover the highest divine quality, namely love.

No other animal can "hope". Only humans can draw from a higher nature the ability to avoid despair by invoking this "four letter word". The strength that we attain from this virtue certainly does not spring from the rational side of our nature. Is it rational to hope in the face of the pains of reality? Or is this ability merely an evolutionary device formatted as a release for our anxiety? No, when we hope we draw from outside our dual mental functions and become truly human.

The cousin of hope is another divine quality, imagination. To hope and dream of things outside our existence is not rational. Ironically, hope and imagination is at the core of rational, scientific thought. In the scientific method, first you frame a hypothesis. Then the hypothesis is tested. By experimentation and observation, scientific theory is developed. But the essence of the process is the first step, the formation of the hypothesis. Where does that thought come from?

Certainly, when the Wright brothers wanted to fly, they invoked the scientific method. They tested their hypothesis

71

time and again by building models, designs, prototypes, until one of their contraptions lifted off at Kitty Hawk. The initial thought that man can fly though was not rational. It was derived from their imaginations, their dreams, and their hope for a better future, adventure or even financial reward. Whatever the reason the spark of creativity that served as the catalyst for this invention was drawn from the higher self.

Courage is another of these fascinating concepts. Rationally it is difficult to understand physical courage. To throw one self into the heat of battle, or in harms way for the sake of another, defies rational self interest. Perhaps physical courage is an evolutionary step derived from the protectiveness of a lioness for her cub, for example, but the exhibitions of physical courage for strangers defy simple explanation from an evolutionary standpoint. More challenging then physical courage is the ability to act in the face of fear on a daily basis. To take the steps necessary to go on, at times seems overwhelming. This ability to continue is neither based in reason or in emotion. We draw from our higher self this courage to face fear, to act against the anxiety inherent in the unknown, and go on. The theologian, Paul Tillich described this trait as the Courage to Be.

Take the desire to persevere, for example. Is it rational to doggedly pursue a course of action in the face of repeated obstacles? Or is this stubbornness, so essential to achievement, in some fashion a trait left over from evolutionary development? I suggest that hope, imagination, and quality would be utterly useless without the ability to bring these concepts to fruition. Hence, we are gifted with the divine quality of perseverance. Without perseverance, the ideas created in our mind through hope and imagination would never come into existence.

Man is a social animal interacting with countless people every day. Each of us unique with interminable mixtures of personality traits, yet, by and large, we survive. There are other divine natures that help us in this task. Empathy is just such a quality. The ability to know at an instant how another person feels is part of the beauty of being human. Not sympathy, that feeling connotes some judgment of the condition of another usually involving pity. But we are capable of sensing as soon as someone looks at you whether they are happy, sad, worried, afraid, or even lonely. Perhaps, this form of human radar evolved from animal instincts, but I believe empathy is derived from the highest levels of caring and quality, and is part of the essence of human existence.

When asked what character attributes were lacking in criminals, psychologists bemoaned the criminal's inability to empathize. The failure to feel, know or care about another person was the greatest defect, state the experts. Having many conversations with other prisoners, I am forced to agree. True criminals lack an understanding of the pain caused to others by them. Take a simple burglary, as an example. Even though no one was home, and no party hurt during the crime, the criminal cannot comprehend the feeling, akin to rape, that the victim feels when they realize that a stranger was in their home.

While some of the important virtues of social intercourse, such as tolerance and respect, can be rooted in rational thought, empathy retains a mystical nature. It is reasonable to tolerate another's differences because we derive a rational benefit. But to know how another is feeling, is truly human radar in action. To care, hope, imagine, empathize and act with courage make us, as humans, unique. When we couple these qualities with our rational abilities, and the power of emotion, our true nature is revealed.

Before leaving this subject, I must mention two other physical characteristics no doubt tied in some fashion to our evolutionary development, but they have divine benefits.

73

Why do we laugh and cry? Both of these diametrically opposed actions release the tensions of life. What a mystical occurrence it was to wire humans for this release. It is as though that somewhere in our development it was known that our expanding mind could not contain the pressures of life. A check valve to release the pain was installed. We laugh and cry, sometimes at the same time, and we feel better.

I recall vividly laying in the top bunk in the Chapel Hill complex of Fort Benning, Georgia. I was in the third week of basic training, and our platoon had just returned from night maneuvers. Drained, dirty and disgusted we bunked down after lights out. We were strangers from all over the country, each with different backgrounds, and physically exhausted after 19 hours of basic training. Suddenly, from one end of the barracks a Northerner yelled a question to a Southern man about the special qualities of Southern women. A voice from my lower bunk, occupied by an Alabama private, yelled something about them being "finger lickin good". From the throes of exhaustion, laughter rang out. Forty strangers laughed so hard that tears came. If there is no God, then I am certainly grateful for the evolutionary course that mandated the release brought by laughter and tears.

Mr. Drummond, or Mr. Darrow, was partially correct in arguing that our ability to think makes us different from all other beings. But the difference is far greater. For to be human and conscious means that mystical qualities were conferred on us. It is our duty to develop and cherish these abilities.

MARRIAGE

"To love another person is to see the face of God."
Les Miserables (the play)

*"He that troubleth his own house
Shall inherit the wind."*
Proverbs 11:29

Not being content with destroying all facets of my professional career, I proceeded to ruin my most valuable asset, namely my marriage. Living with another under the vows of the marriage contract is difficult under normal circumstances. My life, however, was so full of lies and deceit; punctuated with deep compulsiveness that I am surprised my marriage lasted as long as it did. I was fortunate; I married a wonderful, loving women. But there is a limit to the pain that anyone can withstand.

Ironically, of all my failures, the loss of my marriage must top the list. There is no other choice made in life that involves the degree of commitment as living with some one for the rest of your life. The responsibility permeates all levels of existence. It fills all the rational moments and reaches the deepest levels of our emotional being. So too, must the failure cut across all levels. I have spent a great deal of time examining this phase of my failure. Strange, how paradoxical is life. We do so much when we are young, all without knowledge. But by the time we become wise, it is often too late to do anything. We marry without the proper understanding of the commitment.

No marriage is simple. Arguments and problems abound throughout the years. There is suffering and there is joy. At the fateful ceremony, we exchange vows. In this modern era, some of the vows are self-written, but the tried and true is "to love and honor one another until death do us part." There has been a great deal of change in the institution of marriage. Couples marry later in life. The number of children borne is less then in years past. And the rampage of filed divorces has subsided somewhat. Yet the secret to successful marriage remains a carefully buried mystery.

The answer lies in two concepts. The first involves the true meaning of the marriage vow. Love and honor are great concepts, but they do not guide us. When a person agrees to marry another, that person is really saying - "I will be the one there for you." Not that I will be always happy or pleasant. Not that I will always be the groping schoolboy. Not that I will always agree with you. But, of all the people in the world, I will be the one there for you. Those words embody the essence of the commitment made at marriage.

Several years ago my grandmother died. As deaths go, hers was beautiful. She was aged and sick. That day in the hospital, by sheer coincidence, all of her children were by the bed. She passed quietly with her children watching. I left the room to call home, and told my father of my grandmother's death. He asked about my mother. I said she was fine and that I would drive her home. About an hour later, I pulled into the driveway of my parents' house. There by the door way was my father. Understand, that as wonderful as my father was, he would never be mistaken for a Cary Grant. I suppose no child ever pictures their parents as dashingly romantic. Yet his arms were open and my mother rushed to him. He held her as she cried. I realized at that instant the meaning of a long marriage - the true meaning of marriage love. My father was the one person there for my mother. Regardless of the trouble and joy of the years, they were there for each other.

But how do you survive during the day-to-day experiences of being two separate people living together under one roof. Famed trial attorney, Gerry Spence wrote a book entitled How To Argue And Win Every Time. In his chapter on marital communication, I believe he found the magical answer. You win by losing – yes, another paradox. In a successful marriage there are three components. The first two are easy, the man and women. The third is invisible, but more important then the other two parts. It is the relationship. Every time the husband gives in, compromises, loses if you will, and when that compromise is matched by the compromise of the wife, neither party gets what they want. But the relationship grows. In a successful marriage there are no individual victors.

In the late 1960's the divorce laws of New York were amended to recognize grounds for divorce other then adultery. The floodgates of divorce litigation opened. The courtroom in Brooklyn, New York had a makeshift sign over the door announcing that the parties were entering Freedomland. After one bitter proceeding, Justice Louis Heller called me to the bench and asked me whether both parties were angry over his decision. I told the judge that in fact they were both disappointed. "Good", he responded. "Because if one party was happy, then I made a bad decision."

The same analysis is true in a successful marriage. If both parties are somewhat upset about the resolution of a problem, then the relationship is stronger. If one party is happy and the other is not, the relationship has suffered. How many times has this scene played out? The husband wants to watch Monday night football, but the wife, tired from a long day and having no desire to cook dinner, asks to go to the new restaurant that opened. Of course, you know that you can't afford the restaurant she selected because finances are somewhat tight.

It is not hard to imagine that within a few short bursts of conversational invective. The wife is accused of being lazy and a spendthrift. Just as quickly, the husband will be told that he is a lazy, uncaring oaf, with limited financial means that didn't want a wife but a slave. Does any of this sound familiar?

But what if both parties lost? The husband knows that the game is not a playoff contest, and he can leave for more then an hour and still get to see the second half. So he agrees to go, but suggests a cheaper alternative. She, on the other hand, loses as well, saying that the local diner will be fine. Neither party received what they wanted. But the relationship grew. By each party losing, the marriage becomes stronger.

I wish I realized these two truths while I was married. Your spouse is the one you selected to be there for you, and by losing the marriage wins. As one grows older, you recognize that humans were not meant to be alone. We all need someone to be there for us. If you are fortunate enough to find that person who compliments your existence, cherish the privilege.

HOW I SURIVIVED ATTICA

"He who has a why can bear with almost any how"
Nietzsche

Former Chief Judge of the New York Court of Appeals, Sol Wachtler described his prison experience in After the Madness, A Judge's Own Prison Memoir. As frightening as his tale was, Judge Wachtler served only one year in a Federal Prison. He never did time in Attica or Sing Sing. The conclusion of his book, however, was telling. He stated that he was willing to discuss the ills of the prison system with anyone who would listen, but no one was willing. I understand that feeling.

Nassau County decided to sentence me to a term of 7 to 14 years. Whether the term was warranted or not is irrelevant. I did wrong, and must bear the responsibility for my acts. But the particulars of my prison experience are useful to view an underbelly of society. Most may say let the seediness lie buried. Unfortunately, what lies behind those walls is a microcosm of our society. How we deal with the worst, shows how far, or how little, we have as a civilization progressed.

Many books about prison life have been written. Like Judge Wachtler, I too kept a journal. In preparing for this essay, I reviewed many of the daily entries. The faces of my co-felons rushed to my eyes. Some of my acquaintances were notorious, infamous, some extremely violent: all tragic. Tragedy is the basis of the system. The pain of the countless, unnamed victims of the crimes is tragic. So too, is the loneliness and despair of the slamming metal cell door. No chronological recitation of the day-to-day depravity is warranted. Senseless acts took place in each prison I was in, and to fill pages with them satisfy only the prurient. Yet, there are constants that should be revealed.

I served a little more then 6 years in confinement. The last months of my 7-year term were served on a work release program that required me to return to prison in the evenings while working during the day. My confinement was long and hard. But I was blessed. There were times when I could not see the end of the tunnel. I exited the system physically whole though worn. Mentally, I fear the scars do not easily heal. The nightmares continue even now.

My prison life started in the Nassau County jail. At the County level, three classes of prisoners are housed. There are those serving County time, imprisonment on misdemeanor charges or felonies where the term imposed is a year or less. Then there are individuals who have been sentenced to State time, and are awaiting transfer to an upstate facility for processing. Depending upon the overcrowding in the State system, the time for transfer can vary from a few days to several months. The vast majority of individuals in County are awaiting trial or disposition of their cases. These are people who cannot make the bail imposed or have been denied bail. It must be emphasized, however, that the vast majority of those incarcerated at the county level are innocent under the rights contained in our Constitution. Yet, in many aspects this confinement is the cruelest of all.

The facilities available to the prisoners pale in comparison to the State institutions. The law library is inadequate. And it is at the local level where legal research is the most important. Fights break out virtually everyday. Gang allegiance is paramount. Bloodletting is the result of contact between some of the rival factions. The scars of gang battle are worn on the checks of many young men. Often a scar caused at the County level will create more serious consequences when the prisoners reach the State institutions. Many acts of gang violence in the State system are vengeance for slights that took place while prisoners were housed in the County.

In Nassau County we are given orange uniforms to wear. I found it humorous how some of the youth would keep a neatly pressed set of "oranges" to wear for visits. I suppose the young ones did not realize that it was impossible to look good in prison garb; regardless of how many creases you fold into shirt. The food was inedible - simply inedible. I believe I dropped 40 pounds during the 9 months before my transfer upstate.

Then there were the endless transfers between the jail and the courthouse. Up at 5 in the morning, change into your court clothes and then moved to a cell in the bottom of the courthouse. While waiting hours for a court appearance that would last a few minutes, most of the prisoners would take a plea to avoid what is affectionately known as "bullpen therapy". I was amazed how some people had the strength to actually go to trial day after day during this process. How could they remain sharp? How could they concentrate on their case? They couldn't, and the vast majority was found guilty. They never had a chance.

Then one morning in February 1995, at 3AM my cell door cracked, and my stay in Nassau was over. I was on my way to Downstate in Westchester County for processing. Within hours, I became 95 A 1551. I would remain a number until April 30, 2001. At Downstate, prisoners guilty of all types of crime are thrown together for the initial sorting. There are physicals, testing, and interviews with so-called counselors who assist in the classification procedure. I entered the State system with slightly over 6 years remaining on my prison term (In prison parlance the confinement period is called a "bid"). Because my crime was non-violent, the guidelines permitted a classification of medium security. But no, for some reason I was deemed a risk, and classified Maximum security B. Of course for all practical purposes there were no "B" Facilities, so I was assigned a Maximum-security facility that housed the most hardened criminals known to the State of New York. Naturally, I challenged this classification. There was no reason for this action, but not only was my request denied, no intelligent rationale for this classification was ever supplied.

Two weeks after my arrival at Downstate, a mini riot occurred at Sing Sing. While his cell door was supposedly locked, a prisoner was stabbed to death in B block - a very troubling occurrence. In response, the State decided to ship out many of the prisoners residing in Sing Sing to other facilities throughout the state. That is one of the methods used to keep the peace in the system. Keep the prison population moving. Always try to mix up the chemistry in the facility. To be frank, it works. The empty spots had to be filled, and within hours, I approached the wall of Sing Sing. It would take the combined talents of Shakespeare and Hemingway to describe the depressive, frightening sight of the maximum-security concrete wall. I will not try.

Sing Sing has two main blocks aptly called "A" block and "B" block. "A" block has made the Guinness Book of Records as the largest cell block in the world. "B" block is only a few cells behind that classification. Several hundreds of prisoners are housed in various tiers of endless cells. The cellblock is really no more then a huge warehouse, with tiers of cells fitted neatly upon one another. And the noise - it was never ending. As I stated previously, it is not my purpose to recite the endless acts of violence, depravity, drug use and waste that took place during my 6 years of confinement. But I survived. Undoubtedly my legal knowledge was a useful tool. I shared my talents with all who asked. And I worked for free. I never charged for my services. No cigarettes or stamps (both the currency of jail). But more importantly, it was integrity that served as my armor. I learned that the word of an individual was the most important thing, especially when there exists nothing else.

After staying in Sing Sing for 8 months, I was transferred to Attica. That prison outside of Buffalo, New York became renown because of the Attica riot. Attica made Sing Sing look like a summer camp. The wall was red brick with huge medieval parapets spaced at fixed intervals serving as gun towers. My first telephone call was to my sister. I told her that if my mother had any allusions to visit me there, she must talk her out of it. The sight of that place from the outside alone would have killed her.

Two black youths were transferred with me that day. They were all mouth on the way over ranting on how they would bend that jail to their wills. We were met at the gate by a guard who had to be the poster boy for correction officers. He stood 6 foot 7 inches with muscle on muscle. Naturally, he had no neck, and the stick that he held in his arm looked more like a toothpick. Within seconds these two rambunctious types were deadly silent, and probably remained that way for months.

As fate would have it, I was housed in D Block. It was D Block that served as the main location for the riot. I worked as a clerk in the school that adjoined D Block. And of course it was in the school where some of the civilians were taken prisoner. And my recreation was in D Block yard - the very yard where the riot ended in a hail of bullets those many years ago. I have never felt closer to ghosts then those days when I walked the yard.

When we traveled through the halls we did so by the various tiers. Each group would travel the halls in silence, always under the watchful eyes of the CO with nightstick at the ready. The mess hall was a huge marble structure. Undoubtedly, it served as the model for the prison movies of the 1920's. About one half hour before meals the intercom would announce that gas was on the move. That simply meant that the tear gas used in the event of an altercation was being delivered to the mess hall to control the inmates. Even a simple fight could easily blossom into a full-scale riot.

While I was confined, I saw blood. Terrible fights and mini riots in the prison yards. Bodies dropped. If I recall, there were two deaths at Sing Sing, one in Attica and one in Green Haven. All over nonsense. A gold chain, army jacket, small drug debt would easily cost a life in maximum security. The blood continued in medium security. In fact, at one of the jails, Greene County, known for its youthful population, blood flowed often and stupidly. Gang violence was the cause.

Despite the depravity, there were times when there was laughter. People have an uncanny ability to adapt. We are resilient. But every moment was ripe with danger. You never knew when a situation would develop, and you would be caught in the wrong place, at the wrong time. The battles are far too numerous to recite. Through it all my legal ability, sense of integrity, wit and street smarts permitted me to survive those days. Of course, I followed the three no's of prison. – No queers, no drugs and no gambling. But there was something more.

I prayed. I prayed night and day. I prayed for protection, for strength. I prayed that I would find the right people to help me get through this experience. And my prayers were answered. In each of these facilities, although people who committed the most heinous of crimes abound, I found the right group to protect and guide me in a truly foreign environment. Attica was the worst, but it was not the end. From there I was transferred to Green haven, a maximum-security prison that housed the largest percentage of prisoners doing life in the State of New York.

Finally, my classification, still a mystery to me, could no longer maintain a maximum level, and I was transferred to a medium facility. The first was Fishkill. There were still problems and pain. But I felt that my prayers were answered. Somehow I survived. Men, who were criminals, assisted me. But a greater force protected me.

THE CRIMINAL JUSTICE SYSTEM
MORE CRIMINAL THEN JUSTICE

"There is no such thing as justice – in or out of Court."
Clarence Darrow

*"Laws are like cobwebs, which may catch small flies,
but let wasps and hornets break through."*
Jonathan Swift

One of the most frequently asked questions by the few people who are still talking to me concerns the people I met behind the wall. I suppose there is a curious fascination with criminals. "Were any of the prisoners actually innocent?" they ask. I met many prisoners during my travels throughout the State; many notorious, most were not. Because of my legal ability and some success in opening the prison doors for a few, I was inundated with requests to read trial transcripts. I was asked to find some glimmer of hope for many. They would try anything to sustain a new round of applications for reversals or a new trial. The odds against any post conviction relief are so high; any attempt to compute the percentages is a waste of time. But still they tried. You see; hope is one of the magical qualities that make us human. When hope fails all that is left is despair. And it is all too easy to despair behind those walls.

Based on my experience I would say that 98% of those serving time are guilty. Guilty of something, but not necessarily for the crime they are serving. Some of the laws in this State are very confusing. For example, while in Attica I met a man in his late forties. He was in the 23rd year of a 25 to life sentence for murder. While in his late teens, he and two other black youths from Buffalo robbed a candy store. They had no weapons, and homicide was the furthest thing from their minds. As the boys ran from the store, a shot was fired by a chasing policeman. The bullet ricocheted killing a female passerby. New York has a felony murder statute on the books. When someone dies as a result of a felony or in the flight from the scene of the crime, the participants in the crime are jointly liable for murder. The intent to kill anyone is not an element of the crime. In technical parlance, the law creates a legal fiction transferring the criminal intent from the underlying felony, in this instance, the robbery to the murder. Thus, this individual was as guilty as if he had planned the murder of this victim for years and then killed the individual.

These are tough questions. This passerby should not have died. It is more then tragic. Undoubtedly, her death was the result of criminal activity, but was it murder, and did it justify the maximum sentence imposed? The way the prosecution is permitted to join different theories of the crime also creates problems. New York has three types of murder, all under the heading of murder in the second degree. The first involves the normal run of the mill intent to kill. This is the type of homicide that we would ordinarily see on television on the old Colombo's or other detective shows. There are defenses to intentional murder. If the death occurred during a moment of extreme emotional disturbance, for example, the defendant could be spared the murder charge and be found guilty of Manslaughter. Other defenses exist, intoxication for example, which serve to negate the level of intent necessary for intentional murder.

But there is another type of murder - depraved indifference. Here no specific intent to kill need be shown. But if the defendant evinces recklessness and acts under a depraved indifference to human life then a murder charge can lie. Take the example of shooting a rifle in the air. That is reckless, and if the bullet falls and kills someone, a murder charge can ensue. Here is the problem. There are no defenses to depraved indifference. Emotional disturbance does not lower the charge. Intoxication is not a defense. To the contrary, evidence of intoxication goes to bolster the prosecutions case of reckless conduct. The third type of murder is the felony murder law discussed above. All of these types of homicide invoke the same penalty.

The prosecution has the ability to join all the theories of the crime in one indictment. How is the defendant supposed to defend against theories that conflict with one another? I saw too many instances when the defendant was acquitted of intentional homicide but guilty of depraved indifference. Many people were found guilty of the lower manslaughter charge because of emotional disturbance, but also of depraved indifference and the sentence of 25 to life was imposed. Confusing, isn't it?

Also, there were many guilty verdicts that I questioned. Far too many bar fights where there was loss of life were deemed murder, when the combatants were equally involved; alcohol dulling the senses and judgment of all. I reiterate most are very guilty, but not of the degree of criminality assessed. Now, are there innocent people behind those walls? Unfortunately, far too many then we care to admit.

A few cases quickly come to mind. Before I went to work release, I met Mr. Bill. After a trial in Brooklyn, New York, he was found guilty of murdering a bar patron following an argument. He presented two alibi witnesses that swore he was not at the scene that evening. The prosecution had one eyewitness, who identified Mr. Bill as the killer. As too often is the case, that witness was offered a deal and a substantial reduction of the sentence on another charge for his testimony. This was just another case of "black on black" crime, and I am sure it only received a passing note in the papers, if it received any attention at all. At the end of the trial, Bill was found guilty and sentenced to 25 years to life for the murder.

At the end of his 25 years, Bill was denied parole. The reason cited was his failure to recognize the seriousness of his crime. During the parole hearing he exercised his right and denied his guilt. So by invoking his right to deny guilt, he was evidencing a failure to recognize his criminality and thus denied parole. Check the definition of oxymoronic. Two years later he was again denied parole for the same reason. Now it was 29 years after his imprisonment and the Parole Board beckoned again. Before his appearance, he came to see me. I reviewed his case and his record. In 29 years of incarceration, there was not one disciplinary infraction; not one improper notation; not one work report less then exemplary. Also, the time served had affected his health, Bill was seriously ill. I told him that in my opinion, he would have to find a way to admit the crime, and explain his past failure to do so. I was sure that with just such an admission, release would only be weeks away. He looked at me, and tears filled his eyes. "I can't," he said. "I just can't admit to something I did not do." "It would make my life a lie."

When I left that facility, Bill was still there having been again denied release for the third time. And there were others. Advancements in the field of DNA research have emptied many a cell. But the District Attorneys consistently fight to validate convictions regardless of the results of these tests. They find ways to challenge the validity of reports that vindicate the defendant. It requires a Herculean effort to get a judge to even review an application for post conviction relief, let alone grant serious consideration to the merits. Far too often the distinction between justice and winning is lost.

Of course, I will be accused of being a flaming left wing liberal. I believe, however, that my experience as an attorney who tried criminal cases and as a criminal permits a somewhat unique view of the system at work. Let me be clear on this. I am not in favor of crime. I am not pleading the plight of the criminal. The devastation caused by crime cannot be taken lightly. No, what I ask is for the light of intellectual honesty to shine on the system. That is not being a liberal, but being honest. Incidentally, as I have noted elsewhere, labeling political proclivities is merely a communicative trick to invoke emotional response, but believe me, a "right wing" archconservative quickly becomes liberal if he is ensnared in the trap of the system.

The criminal justice system, as imperfect as it is, is the crown jewel of all our Constitutional protections. The protections afforded in the Fourth, Fifth, and Sixth Amendments to the Constitution as applied to the States in the Fourteenth Amendment were a direct result of our founding fathers' fear of governmental power and intrusion. Procedural checks, roadblocks to unbridled governmental action, were imbedded in these amendments. The words contained in these guarantees, such as probable cause, right to counsel, self-incrimination protection, have been interpreted endlessly by the Supreme Court. At the core of these words lies the foundation of the criminal justice system, namely fundamental fairness. If the system was fundamentally fair then the potential for improper governmental intrusion is checked, and the playing field between the state and the defendant is level. As admirable as the concept of fairness is it also contains the root of the problem. The sensitivities of the citizenry are assuaged by the fairness of the system. The correctness of the result is secondary.

If the procedural protections are afforded, the conviction stands. It makes no difference if the party is guilty or not. Further, it is extremely easy to provide the procedural protections. People complain about the protections afforded the criminal. The liberal Supreme Court decisions of the 1960's that gave rise to the Miranda warnings, and the right to counsel, have been criticized as handcuffing the ability of police to do their job. Guilty people are being released in droves because of procedural loopholes argue the uniformed masses. Yet, the State enters guilty pleas by negotiation or by trial in nearly 95% of the arrests. And an extremely high percentage of these convictions are based upon confessions or admissions that do not run afoul of the Miranda protections. Recently, our current Supreme Court has been struggling with the relationship between our Constitutional guarantees and a claim of innocence. Innocence is not a protected right. Apparently, someone who is innocent of the crime must find a Constitutional violation before they can obtain a review of the conviction. Being innocent may not be enough.

The underlying concept is simple. Our criminal court is supposed to be a battleground for truth. The adversary system pits the prosecuting attorney against the defense counsel. The procedural safeguards in the Constitution level the playing field against the power of the government. The verdict of the 12 impartial jurors determines the fate of the accused. Our system is the best created by man, but since it is created by man, it is imperfect. Innocent people do get convicted. Of that fact there can be no doubt. One reason, as I mentioned, is the emphasis upon procedural niceties as opposed to the certitude of guilt, and the second is the vast number of lies.

In court everyone lies. The prosecuting attorneys place on the stand police officers that they know are lying. The State stretches the bounds of procedural disclosure to ensure that only the most minimal of materials need be presented to the defense. For obvious political purposes, press conferences attesting to the guilt of the accused before any trial fill the papers and airwaves. I was always amazed how virtually every arrest conforms to the procedural requirements of the Constitution. It is the rare case, or perhaps the non-existent case, when a Police Officer admits that he failed to give the required Miranda warnings after the arrest.

The defense is no slouch when it comes to creating imaginative mendacities. Phony alibi witnesses appear from nowhere. Defendant's testimony neatly tailored to circumvent certain elements of the crime. It is a miracle that juries can sort out soiled testimony and arrive at a verdict at all. Ironically, the jury system is a most remarkable invention. In my experience those 12 people who have never before met, once they take the oath truly attempt to do justice. On those occasions when they are wrong, it often is not their fault. The failure lies in either an over zealous prosecution or inept defense.

Judges, as well, must bear some responsibility for the state of the criminal justice system. Those who wear the black robes have the highest duty. They are the last bastions of protection for the citizenry. Their burden is to balance the needs of society with the individual rights of the defendant. The law, and their duty, nothing else, must motivate them. Unfortunately, those who ascend to the bench do so as a result of the political process. Too often, that process can exert pressure on the Courts. When Judges exclude evidence or if the Courts release a defendant because of a Constitutional inadequacy, they are not pro-criminal. They are pro-Constitution. We all should fear Judges closing their eyes to our protections because of their belief as to the guilt of a defendant.

In the late 1980's the population demanded control of their streets. They had a right to do so, and as a result the "get tough on crime" adage came to the forefront. In the 1990's, the various segments of the criminal justice system were falling over one another to see who could be the toughest. Tough new laws were passed in the legislatures of the States and United States Congress. District Attorneys refused to negotiate pleas. The sentencing was harsher. More prisons to warehouse people were needed. Once a defendant was confined, Parole Boards, as if in a spirit of not to be out done, refused to release inmates regardless of their rehabilitative record. That is, of course, if parole was not abolished once and for all. Appellate courts decided to add to the toughness by narrowing procedural protections or if there were error in the trial they would deem it "harmless" and permit the convictions to stand. Congress limited access to the Federal Courts by reducing the availability of the greatest protection we have, the Writ of Habeas Corpus, and for the most part the Federal Courts quietly acquiesced. This pressure was evident with the election, or appointment, of trial judges noted for their limiting view of the Constitution, and their assurance to be tough on crime.

Politics and public opinion does not belong in the Courthouse. The greatness of our civilization does not rest in polls, but in the realization that our system of justice supplants the desires of the defendant or the wants of the victim. It exists on a higher plane. Those protections afforded in the Bill of Rights stand as a barrier between the lynch mob borne of vengeance, and governmental force resulting from a call for security. The balance is tenuous. Our freedom demands that the balance be respected, and even cherished.

Frank M. Manfredi

WHY DO GOOD PEOPLE
DO BAD THINGS

*"What you now need is not a return to morality,
but to discover it."*
<u>Atlas Shrugged</u>, Ayn Rand (Galt's speech)

*"Anyone can become angry-that is easy-but to be angry,
with the right person, to the right degree, at the right time,
for the right purpose-this is not easy."*
Aristotle

On any day, just look at a newspaper. Whether on a national or local level, the headlines are replete with tales of normally good people committing some form of transgression. There is no shortage of sex scandals, untold acts of greed, with the occasional mindless act of violence thrown in. How many countless people have been affected by one split second of stupidity? Human tragedy for both the victims and victimizers flows from these failings. We must realize there are always victims. Even if the mistake goes unnoticed by others, you become the victim of your own stupidity. In fact, we need not have to look at the news for evidence of bad acts. Our own lives are full of many examples. We lie. We cheat. We violate our marriage vows. We destroy the trust that others have placed in us. We can become irresponsible, and fail to do what we know we should do.

Why do good people do bad things? This is truly an age old question. It stems from the deep philosophical argument as to the nature of man. Is man inherently good or bad? I have always been fascinated by Plato's discussion of the problem in the "Ring of Gyges" contained in The Republic. In one section, Plato writes of a dialogue

94

between Socrates and Glaucon. Glaucon tells the tale of a shepherd named Gyges, who finds a magical ring on a statue. When wearing the ring he is able to turn himself invisible. How will the human act when cloaked with this power of invisibility? Will he be moral or not? In the tale, the evil side wins with Gyges seducing the Queen and murdering the King of Lydia. The tale was told to show that despite the best of intentions, when permitted, the evil side of man seeps to the forefront. Perhaps this ancient interpretation is correct. For as I have noted elsewhere, our animal side is far more ancient then our ability to reason, and that animal side is responsible for many of our failings; many, but not all.

Would we act properly absent the existence of laws, or were these bodies of rules enacted by society, in some sober moment, to protect us against ourselves? Or do these laws actually reflect man's higher nature, and the ability to live together in peace and harmony? I certainly can ask many questions, the answers, however, are difficult. One thing is certain. The vast majorities of people do not desire, nor intend, to do evil. Yet, it happens. Even most of the prison population consider themselves good, and they deny repeatedly their intention to do evil. Although most police would argue that the criminal intended only not to get caught.

The inability to control our base emotions is an obvious, albeit too easy, answer to the question raised. The force of anger, whether raised by threat, envy, jealousy is powerful indeed. When we act solely out of anger, we normally regret the consequences. Clearly, when we are driven by our base emotions, our passions if you will, bad things result. In the battle between the rational mind, and the emotions, the emotions always seem to win. Previously, I have talked about the necessity of a strong value structure to provide that momentary break necessary to permit the rational part of our brain to kick in. If we have a problem with unbridled emotion, then a transformation is necessary. The value structure must be put into place that will permit a breather for the passion to dissipate even slightly so that bad action will not follow.

But, as noted, unbridled emotion is too easy an answer. Why would a lawyer or accountant suddenly steal money that was entrusted to him? Why would a cleric engage in deviant sexual behavior? Why would a spouse cheat on someone that they love? You can add your own countless examples of good people engaging in bad behavior.

As in all phases of our existence, there is a conflict between two forces that causes much of the problem. The greatest need of a person is to be liked by others or to be accepted. No doubt, this social intercourse is a vital element of what makes us human. The trap, however, is defining what validates our individual existence. If what we are is determined by outside forces problems develop. When we validate our existence by the approval of others or by the material things we have within our possession, our concept of self whether it be self-love, self-esteem, or self image is drawn from without, not within. That picture of who we are is fragile, and when challenged by the realities of life, our base brain reads the challenge as an attack. Just as an animal will fight for survival, so too will our limbic brain start our survival process in a mere instant. Our emotions will rush to heal the crack in our veneer either by attack or avoidance – fight or flight.

But that animal instinct, so valuable in eons gone by, only causes more harm. The attacks we face in today's world are not normally attacks on our survival, but attacks on the erroneous pictures of ourselves drawn from validation that occurs from outside. That is why I consider the only true definition of self to be self worth. That characteristic creates a picture based on internal forces. The validation comes from within, and not from without. It is another view of integrity. Being integral, or whole is one of the definitions of that virtue. Although acceptance and approval of others is important, it is not controlling when one has a firm handle on his integral worth.

Let me try to be specific. Perhaps 85% of the male population of prison is there because of the involvement at some level of a woman. I would assume that the percentages are the same in the female side of the institution. Perhaps, the acts may not involve a woman directly, but the prisoner acted stupidly either to impress a lady, or to obtain money for a lady, or to increase his image by acquiring things, even drugs, to secure ladies. That is a reality. That prisoner defined his existence by the women around him or by the material things he acquired. When the prisoner did not have these items, he deemed it an attack on his existence, and he responded either by fight to acquire them, or by flight to avoid the consequences of his acts to acquire them.

I am not against acquiring beautiful cars, jewelry or having a handsome lover. But when their approval controls your actions or they are the only reason for your existence, you are hollow inside. When you lose that approval, pain is the result. And from our earliest days as humans, we are wired to avoid the pain. We medicate the pain by turning to drugs or alcohol. We create compulsions to avoid the pain, such as fits of shopping, over eating, misuse of money, and the dreaded sexual compulsion. (To be blunt, that one I never have fully understood). We would lie, cheat, and steal if needed to avoid facing that pain. But facing the pain is an imperative. It must be accepted as a necessity of life, not avoided.

Life also throws us another peculiar curve when we act badly. Unless we are truly psychopathic we all have consciences. That little voice that tells us we are about to step out of the bounds of proper behavior. What creates that voice is the subject for psychological controversy. Unquestionably it is honed by our values and upbringing,

97

thus a result of nurturing. But I believe it is also part of consciousness, and the existence of the mental cop, if you will, is contained deep in our DNA. Regardless, it is there. Depending upon the perceived threat to our existence, our limbic brain will set in motion forces that will easily sweep aside that voice to a mere whisper.

The curve that life throws is that when we are out of bounds for the first time, we seldom if ever get caught. It is almost as though that the first transgression was a freebee. Yet, the mental voice becomes weaker with each passing transgression. Soon the pleasure of our acts, or the avoidance of the pain deadens even the most vitriolic conscience. The inappropriate response becomes an automatic mechanism, and actually can become a part of our personality. Think about it. Were we caught on our first lie? Didn't the lying become easier? When we cheated, were we caught the first time? Didn't each subsequent liaison become easier?

Every day, good people do bad things. It is a result of the inability to control our emotions, coupled with improper validation of our existence. This explanation may seem to be, perhaps, just words. Now let me turn to the most difficult of these essays, explaining what happened to me.

WHAT HAPPENED TO ME

"FACILIS DESCENSUS AVERNO"
Easy is the descent into hell

"The imposter syndrome - I know it well. Inside every self assured
professional lives a frightened neurotic who prays that he can some how
succeed before his clients discover the fraud. It's the guilty secret
that drives us all."

DEGREE OF GUILT
Richard North Patterson

This has to be the toughest essay to write. It is obviously difficult to be objective when reviewing your own life. Those who know me would, perhaps, proffer a different view of my downfall. But there were many lonely hours in prison, all spent in thought and regret. I believe it is important to pass on a few insights. Not as a memoir, the particulars of each act of stupidity would require another book, but to highlight the depths to which one can fall. I believe I was a good person who acted very badly. My conduct was criminal, and hurtful to many innocent people. I destroyed my family. I injured others who placed their trust in me. And I sinned against my talents. Why?

What causes more difficulty in life, an addiction or a compulsion? In many respects, this question is similar to asking which caliber of gun can cause more destruction. I never used drugs. Nor was I anything more then a social drinker. Gambling was never my forte. In fact, while in prison I was asked to take part in a card game, or football pool. I joked that I only gambled once in my life and look

99

where it got me. Many times, I wish I were an addict. To those who loved me, my behavior could be more easily explained by my addiction. They could focus on the drugs, alcohol or gambling, and understand my behavior by blaming these outside forces. Not having an addiction, my bad actions became all the more perplexing.

Compulsions are more troubling then addictions. As severe as drug addiction is, the thing, be it a drug, alcohol, gambling or sex that is the instrument of addiction serves as a focus of therapeutic treatment. Once controlled, then the root causes can be addressed. But with compulsions, there is no outside item on which to focus. The compulsion surfaces in far too many different ways. And the most difficult problem is that the compulsive behavior becomes so intertwined in one's personality that it is impossible to distinguish who you are without the compulsive characteristic. For example, if someone is a compulsive liar, the lying becomes so inherently a part of the person that he lives the lie. If someone were a compulsive manipulator, then the act of manipulating others becomes an integral part of the personality of the individual. This becomes the way the compulsive person survives against the problems of daily living. It almost requires radical surgery to strip away the cause of the compulsion, and what is left of the person can become frightening.

There is a further problem in discussing addictions or compulsions. A great deal of controversy exists as to whether these problems are a disease. Therapeutic groups, such as Alcoholics Anonymous and other 12 step programs, cling to the disease modality. It is essential to their method of treatment. Personally, I have a great deal of trouble with this concept, because inherent in the connotation of disease is an element of excuse. If someone suffers a physical disorder, a disease, then the actions are in part excused. The physically disabled, for example, may be unable to work, but society forgives the failure. Perhaps the pain of the sufferer, because of his physical ailment, is severe on a particular day, and he is curt or gruff with others. We are more inclined to forgive the slight and blame the disease. The sufferer generally bares no stigma. And, in fact, often garners sympathy. Our senses permit us to validate the pain and the torment of the sufferer.

Not so for the addict or the compulsive. To society, our senses fail to discern any defect. There does not appear to be any causation for the irrationality. To its credit, science has made great strides in determining a physiological basis for addictive or compulsive behavior. We have learned of dopamine and serotonin imbalances in the brains of addicts. But are still uncertain as to whether these imbalances are the cause or effect of the addictive behavior. The so-called "pleasure" gene has been identified. Yet, its existence does not dictate addictiveness, but at best reveals only a proclivity towards that behavior. Medical science has not identified any virus, bacteria or defective gene that is the cause of this disease. Nor has it identified any medical treatment similar to an antibiotic that can assist in curing or controlling the disease. No wonder society views the addict with skepticism.

But if bones can break, and the vessels surrounding the heart muscle tear, why is so difficult to believe that the greatest organ within our body, our brain, can fail to function properly at times. Mental disease is a reality. The problem is that science has not created a complete picture of the magical qualities of our thoughts and consciousness itself. The ultimate question is similar to the chicken or the egg controversy. Physiologically, we know that our brain is comprised of fluids containing various chemical compounds. Electric current flows through the synapses. When we think there is an increase in the flow of current. But what comes first. Does the thought create the electric response? Or is the thought the result of the electric activity. On our level of reality, understanding cause and effect is imperative. If by chance, the thought results from the increased electrical activity, then what created the impulse for the increased electric activity in the first place.

Until science resolves the riddle, if it can, those suffering from debilitating mental problems will always be viewed askew by those not similarly affected. Epithets such as "character defect", "moral deficiency", "lack of responsibility", "criminal thinking", "laziness", and the one I always personally enjoyed, "you always had a choice" will constantly be spoken sotto voce about the afflicted.

Regardless of the questions of addiction and compulsion, humankind has another fascinating trait. I believe that we all have within ourselves the ability to self-destruct. As we look around we see talented people falling from pinnacles. Untold people unable to deal with their successes turn to drugs or alcohol, or engage in other self-destructive activity. Often those on the pinnacle all so full of hubris, that arrogance fills their existence. In their own minds, they become superior to those around them, as they look down on the little people. Funny, though, how the forces of life seem to catch up with them as well.

I have avoided dealing with me, but I believe the questions raised warrant some thought. In my circumstance, I never believed there would be a problem. I graduated from law school, after a very successful academic career. Married to a woman whom I loved, my future was a blueprint for success. I chose to start a small law firm, and worked hard in those early years. The clients came. And although there were financial concerns, the future of our practice was never in doubt. Slowly my problem developed. I never saw it coming. As I am writing this I am taken aback with the level of my irrationality. Oh, I know all the psychological reasons, but knowing and changing are two different things.

I craved the adulation of my clients. I craved the acceptance of others. I needed the love of those around me.

I feared the loss of that adulation, and would do anything to avoid the loss. I stole, cheated, and lied to avoid losing the acceptance or adulation of anyone who sought my help. There was no "me" just "them". And by pleasing "them", I thought "me" was a better person. There is irony in compulsions. Another paradox, if you will. The more one craves adulation, the less he obtains. The more one needs the love of others the less he receives, and whatever degrees of love he is fortunate enough to have received will in the end be lost. My entire existence, my validation came from the acceptance by others. I never knew who or what I was - until it was far too late.

It is easy for a person's moral compass to become twisted. After my first brush with the law, although the imprisonment was minimal, my loss was great. The inability to practice law was a severe blow. Any rational man would have evaluated the loss, the suffering, and have been grateful for the second chance. Compulsions, however, are strong. Ironically, intelligence acts against you. I consistently denied that I had a problem. I attempted to secure help, but my effort was halfhearted at best. I simply could not believe that someone as intelligent or educated as I could have a problem. Or if I did have a problem, certainly, with my intellect I could control the situation. As the Bible aptly states, "Pride goeth before a fall." In a few years, my hands tightly cuffed behind my back, I was committed to the 7 to 14 year prison term.

The 12 step program defines insanity as doing the same thing over again and expecting a different result – a perfect definition. Why if I lied and destroyed my life would I expect my next set of lies to bring me a different result? So much for the effect of intelligence. There were two faces to my own particular brand of insanity. Both sides involve the concept of fear. Lawyers and problem solvers in general are looked upon as mini-miracle workers. You have a problem, and we attempt to move heaven and earth to solve it. Perhaps this view is idealistic, but it is the basis of the helping professions. When someone came to me with a problem, I accepted the challenge. Obviously, the client, friend or family member was happy. He thought I was great. In turn I felt important and validated. Unfortunately, as life dictates, not all problems can be solved. But when the time came to face the realities, I could not disappoint someone who placed their trust in me.

First, to do so I risked the withdrawal of approval, adulation and love. I was afraid of that loss, because without that rush of approval, I was nothing. I would have to admit that I failed. Since my values of worth came from what the others thought about me, to admit failure was impossible. If I did discuss the realities, often they involved pain to my client or friend. Worse then the withdrawal of acceptance, I was also afraid of any response. Anger at my failure, I surmised would be the response, and I was afraid of his display of anger. I was afraid to say – no. I was afraid to disappoint because of the withdrawal of adulation, and seeing the anger of another.

When faced with this situation, my mind would automatically race. I would diffuse the disappointment and potential anger by lying. Thus everything important to me was preserved, if for only a moment. With every falsehood, the lies came easier.

Many of the problems of those who came to me involved money. If someone needed help and money would solve the problem, the danger multiplied. Of course, "no" was the appropriate response, but this person trusted me to help; to solve their problems. I could not face the anticipated loss of adulation or anger, and would steal from others who entrusted sums to me in order to please the individual currently before me. Go ahead; say it. Crazy?! Nuts! Yet the problem I have just described is common in varying degrees to many people. Think about the compulsiveness of adulation the next time you see some superstar entertainer on the stage. It is as corruptive as any drug, and consumes your personality. My only saving grace is the knowledge that I acted without greed and veniality. Regardless, intent is irrelevant. I laid devastating destruction in my wake.

To those who know me personally, the description of my problems will be very confusing. Trust me; my compulsions were real, and debilitating. A disease? – That delineation is irrelevant. I had the opportunity to effectuate a moral course correction. I had the ability to draw upon the gifts nature provided to humankind to change. I failed in my responsibility to do so. Just another of my failures.

Frank M. Manfredi

SO YOU SCREWED UP
– NOW WHAT?

"A life spent in making mistakes is not only more honorable
but more useful then a life spent doing nothing."
George Bernard Shaw

"Harvard makes mistakes too, you know.
Kissinger taught there."
Woody Allen

Just in case you were wondering, you can follow every piece of advice I offer, and still make mistakes. We are imperfect, and despite the best of intentions, we leave a path strewn with our errors. If you are a player in the game of life, then mistakes will result. Of course, if you choose not to be in the game, then don't be concerned. Precisely, what constitutes a "mistake"? The dictionary defines the word as an action or statement that by reason of faulty judgment, lack of knowledge, or inattention results in a wrong.

Note well, your intent is irrelevant. A mistake is the end result. The wrong can run the gambit from a simple act of negligence borne from mere inattention, to the shredding of documents in the face of Federal investigation, ala Arthur Anderson, in the Enron debacle. In a simple act of negligence, for example, you may not have intended to cause an accident but the dent in the car exists anyway. But intent is important in determining just how great the mistake was. The more venial the intent then the greater the wrong becomes, and therefore the larger the mistake. We all know that mistakes can run from the inconsequential to the large "screw up." My mistakes, because of the repetitive nature, and the unmistaken fact that I should have known better exceed screw-up and reach the f/u category.

The real question is not how to minimize the making of mistakes, although that is a result to be desired, but how to minimize the effect of our errors by proper responses to them. The negative effects of mistakes have an uncanny ability of ballooning depending what we do or fail to do once the mistake is recognized. History is replete with examples of political folly once the cover up of a mistake is embarked upon. Just remember Watergate, Iran-Contra, and the infamous sex/no-sex distinction of the Clinton - Lewinsky entanglement.

One of the more comical responses to an embarrassing error occurred in the movie, Best Little Whorehouse in Texas. In one scene a politician of local renown was found under the sheets with one of the residents of the house. With scandal filling the air, the politician went on television the next day, to calmly state that he had no idea how he got under the sheets with that women of ill repute. He announced that he was drugged and used as part of a Communist plot to discredit him and taint the fine work he was performing for his constituents. His response to the mistake was a perfect example of the big lie.

All right, you have made a mistake, now how do your respond. First, analyze the error. If no one was hurt from the mistake except you, or if to reveal the error would cause some other person harm, be quiet. Find out what you did wrong. Where was your judgment faulty? Did you have sufficient information or were you just careless? Learn from the error and then let it pass. Generally, no constructive purpose will be served by disclosing such a minor error.

Ah, but life is not so generous. Too often our errors cause harm to others, and they receive pain or suffer loss from our mistakes. Of course, under such circumstances you could use the technique of the politician and claim a nefarious plot by others to discredit you. Or you could simply deny your involvement in the error. As you read this you already know the correct course of action. If you hide this type of mistake; if you attempt to cover up; if you ignore the consequences of the mistake; if you lie as to your involvement, the problem will multiple in geometric proportions.

Why do we find it difficult to admit to others our mistakes? Simply such an admission attacks our self image, and we go to great lengths to defend that image. Also we become fearful of the responses of the others to our failings. To admit a mistake is to invite criticism, pain, and the disappointment of others. On this point, I am absolutely certain. The more you ignore the consequences of a mistake, the longer the effect will fester like a sore, and it will continue to cause pain in your life. Remove the sore immediately.

As before, first analyze the error. Learn precisely what you did wrong. What steps could you take to avoid the repetition of the error? Then go to the person injured by your error. Accept the responsibility, and reveal to the appropriate party what occurred; not in piecemeal portions that are the solace of the politician, but totally. By accepting the responsibility for your mistake, and laying out completely the extent of the situation you have created, the effect of the error is lessened. Since everyone makes mistakes, there is no reason to be masochistic in your behavior. But if an apology is in order, do so sincerely. If Nixon had admitted the transgressions of Watergate at the beginning he would have served out his second term. It is perplexing, how we somehow believe that by lying and covering up we preserve some false sense of self. In the end, we fall further.

There are some mistakes that are more difficult to handle. Take my situation, for example. I was guilty of repetitive conduct caused by compulsive behavior. I needed help, but denied that fact. I needed to turn to someone to assist me in resolving my situation, but I did not. That failure only compounded my error. If you find yourself trapped, end the pain. Turn to someone close to you and ask for help.

On the other hand, if you have a friend that turns to you for assistance because of their problems and mistakes. Please help. Save the individual from drowning in their own human failings. Remember, there are two things the person does not want to hear. The first is "How could you?" and the second is "Why did you". Both of those statements have the effect of putting off the one seeking help. It is hard enough to ask for help, and the task should not be made more difficult. If you choose to help, withhold your judgment until the problem is addressed in some fashion. There will be plenty of time to ask those questions, and find the answers.

As you may have gathered, I am partial to movies - the older the better. Although the medium is primarily geared for entertainment, some bits of wisdom emerge from time to time. Take the movie, based upon the Bernard Malamud novel, The Natural, for example. The hero, Roy Hobbs, portrayed by Robert Redford, is confined to a hospital bed. An old gunshot wound became irritated threatening to sideline him from the final game of the series. And with the inability of Hobbs to play, the championship hopes of the team are in dire peril. In his youth, destined to be the greatest ball player of all time, Hobbs made his mistake. He sought the pleasure of a lovely lady draped in black. Unfortunately, she was on a mission to destroy the best people in various fields, and she placed a bullet in the side of Hobbs before ending her own life. Hobbs went down hill after that, eventually resurrecting his career as an old rookie.

On the hospital bed, Hobbs bemoans his mistakes and the current status of his life. His girlfriend from his

boyhood days is there by his bedside. She is known as the
lady in white. Syllogisms abound in Malamud's work. She
gently and in a consoling fashion offers her own view on
life. It seems we have two lives, she states. The one we
learn with and the one we have to live with after that.

Mistakes are the way we learn. Try as we might, we
cannot go back and undo anything. But we can go on. I
trust your mistakes will not reach the level of Roy Hobbs,
and certainly don't permit them to reach the number or the
severity of my errors. To be sure, the mistake may
rearrange the path of your life. Go on. Take the new path
with unbridled enthusiasm and go on.

Mistakes are human. How you resolve the problems
created by the mistakes challenges us to use our best
attributes. Place our fears and self image concerns on hold.
Act with responsibility and honesty, and the mistake will be
placed in its proper perspective. Lie, deceive, and cover up,
suddenly the actual mistake is unimportant, your action
after the mistake will become the larger issue.

CAN YOU HAVE BOTH WEALTH AND INTEGRITY?

*"The real measure of your wealth is
how much you'd be worth if you
lost all your money"*

Anonymous

Money is such a strange thing. We work endless hours, fly from one end of the globe to another in search of promotion, power, and a growing bank account. We are blessed to live in a system where financial growth is possible, if not expected. Millionaires, today, are commonplace. We have families, and desire the best for our children, and comfort for ourselves. Money is an essential ingredient for material advancement. Yet, all the wealth in the world provides no solace when looking at a sick child. Since I have no money, I must be careful. Certainly, any criticism I voice over the pursuit of "dollars" is subject to a charge of "sour grapes."

There is no problem with the pursuit of money. The accumulation of wealth is not a crime. The only valid question is whether a vast financial accumulation can be obtained without violating the philosophy of integrity, honor, and quality. I am constantly reminded of the first women to run for national office as a vice-presidential candidate. Geraldine Ferraro was a New York Democratic politician. She ran a hard. but doomed campaign. Not only was she the first women to run for such high office, she was Italian-American, and a New Yorker. The spotlight was constantly on her and her family.

Her husband, Nicholas, earned his millionaire status from the real estate market in New York. Sure enough, after the defeat in the general election, the limelight found a few cracks in the family financial picture. It seems that some of the mortgages obtained by Nicholas to finance his empire contained exaggerated numbers. The bold, but small, print on the bottom of application forms warns us that any false statements are punishable as a crime. Millions of Americans have exaggerated on these filings. But for the husband of a vice-presidential candidate the scrutiny was unbearable and criminal charges followed.

Mr. Zaccaro's (they had different last names) money was first generation wealth. By that I mean he earned the millions during his lifetime - a respectable feat, no doubt. But I have always believed that no wealth accumulated during the first generation could completely sustain the spotlight of close investigation. It takes a few generations for the money to become clean. The Carnegies, Rockefellers, Fords and the rest of the industrial captains of history were ruthless business men. Corners were cut. Deals made. Wealth accumulated. Now foundations administer their holdings with a view to dispense charity and advancement. Perhaps, it is a form of penance. In any event, the wealth is "clean" and respectable.

There is an exception, however, to my view of first generation wealth. That involves the fortunes made by businessmen who have taken their idea public and have profited by the risk. It is one of the miracles of our system, that any individual with a creative idea, a creative concept, can obtain financing through the issuance of stock. And if the idea bears out, vast wealth can result. Just think of the Bill Gates scenario. Of course, there are critics that would charge that even these advancements took place through ruthless action. Nevertheless conceptually, wealth with integrity can take place in this fashion. But note, there are two concepts involved, a creative idea and risk taking.

Recently, I took part in one of the many "team" meetings so prevalent in our corporate culture. Chairing this particular session was the President of our company. Dynamic, forceful and wealthy he is the picture of a successful businessman. After the meeting ended, I went down the hall to answer a call of nature. Bathroom key in hand, I turned to enter a shorter hallway where the bathrooms were located. There stumbling with his own key was the president. I was trapped. My boss said, "Are you coming in?" I nodded stupidly and followed him. I never realized how equalizing a bathroom can be. There a multimillionaire and a failure were taking care of bodily functions. The president entered the stall. Obviously, he intended a somewhat longer stay. Recognizing that this environment did not bode well for corporate advancement, I chose the stand up equipment.

Through the closed stall door, I heard a voice asking me how I was doing in the company. I responded in a nervous murmur that I was doing as well as can be expected. I commented that he had put together an interesting array of talented individuals. "Well", I heard through the stall door, "that is how you win." I wished him a good day, and after a quick rinse of the hands, exited with a sigh of relief. But all the way back to my shared cubicle (When I think of the private offices of my past, oh well) the word "win" kept repeating in my mind. Win! – is that what business and money is about? Does the money flow to the winners, and the scraps to the losers?

We are competitive beasts. This desire to be the best and better someone or something comes from the depth of our animal nature. Inherent in winning, though, is that there is losing. Sporting events are a perfect example. They channel this competitive urge. The masses that watch those games marvel in the competitiveness, and gloat in the violence inherent in some sports. These events serve a useful purpose. It is as though our animal nature is transferred to the players on the field. They fight the battles for us. And we revel, in the excitement. Yet, our society demands more. The more competitive the culture, the greater the need to win, and the American existence, be it economic, political or social, is the definition of competitiveness.

Is business or earning money nothing more then a reflection of our animal instincts? To be sure, from the competitive desire comes fine attributes. Ambition and achievement, to name just two, flow from competition. But I argue that competition against one person and another or between one company and another is hollow. The victory quickly loses its splendor. Another battle waits the next day. Winning is not the answer. Interestingly, the business environment recognizes the problem with winning. In the realm of corporatespeak, the "win-win" concept has been introduced to negotiations. Under this theory, business arrangements or "deals" can be obtained based upon mutual benefit. In reality, however, I suggest that the win-win works in public, but behind closed doors most still strategize on how to obtain the best for themselves or their company.

What gives meaning to our search for wealth is not competition but creation. Creating is the mystery, and taking a risk is the required action. That is the meaning of a "quality" business or a career based upon quality and integrity. Never compete with anyone other than yourself. Never permit your company to compete with any other entity other than itself. Always, always create. Competition and winning reflects the animal in us, but creating reflects the essence of our humanness, dare I say it, the godliness in us.

But creating is only part of the puzzle. Prudent risks must be taken to bring the creation to reality - from the laboratory to the market, if you will. Take Edison, for example, no one can doubt the brilliance of the creation that became the electric light. But if that light shone only in his laboratory, what end would have been served. To bring that light to the public, risks had to be taken. And in taking those risks further creations were necessary. The electric dynamo needed to power the light came from that risk. As I mentioned elsewhere, price paying is the charge that life inflicts for success. Risk involves being able to pay the price. If you create and are willing to pay the price then you have quality. If wealth follows, which it should, it will be based on the highest of values, and not on the defeat of anyone.

None of us may be an Edison. So how do we create in our daily routine? If we are living a life of caring and quality, the opportunity for creation flows to us. Perhaps, we can find a new way to assist a customer. Maybe, by acting in a caring fashion we create a better work environment. Do we need to take risks as well? Yes, suppose you have found a way to help that customer. Your creation must be formulated and reported to your superior. That involves risk. The boss may think you are an idiot, or he may welcome the suggestion. What ever the result, the creation needs a risk to make it public.

At the opposite end of the spectrum from "price paying" is the term "balance". There is a conflict between the Western mind and the traditions of the Eastern cultures. Balance is so necessary for a happy existence, argues the Easterner. Many management gurus echo the same goal. It would be so wonderful to harness the creative energy, risk taking and price paying with the harmony of a balanced existence. Family, home, community, and work all in perfect balance absent stress. That is a fairy tale. Some part of our existence must suffer when we chose to pay the price for taking a risk. Of course, we need fun and vacations. To enjoy periods of recreation really "recreates" us. Family is important. But anyone who believes they can have it all is kidding themselves. Something must suffer. In fact, perhaps nothing great was ever accomplished without a single minded purpose. Fortunately, we have the choice. Surely, look for the balance in our lives. But don't expect to achieve it. Remember no one on their deathbed says they wished they spent more time at the office.

But if you choose to accumulate money and wealth through creation and quality, and are willing to pay the price, then you have had a quality existence. There will be regrets in anything we do. That is one of the costs of price paying.

The question at the start of this essay was whether we can obtain wealth and integrity at the same time. The answer is a resounding yes, because the wealth is obtained through integrity, through quality, through creativity. The wealth can come from all the attributes that make our humanness so special.

WHAT IS IT ALL ABOUT?

"There are more things in heaven and earth, Horatio,
Than are dreamt of in our philosophy"
Hamlet (Act I Scene V)

I believe that failures have authored the greatest clichés. Who ever coined the phrase that "Money isn't everything," certainly was not a wealthy man. Here is another saying, "Life is a glorious mystery." I suppose that failures have more time on their hands, and are able to spend that time in somber thought. After all the reflection, however, perhaps life is to be lived, not understood. Yet, it is our nature to ask why. Thanks to the scientific method, we have learned the "how" of many things, but not yet the "why". And we, as humans, constantly ask "why". Certainly, my pitiful attempts to give answers to the "why", pale when compared to the volumes of deep thought on the various subjects. I intended, however, only to give some guidance derived from the depths of my failure.

When I discuss my thoughts with others, I have been challenged as postulating a depressing, negative view of life. I have often wondered whether I am allowing my personal depressed state to color my thinking on the subject of life. No, I am not negative on life. To the contrary, I believe the book of life instructions that I have outlined is based on the inexplicable currents of reality. The basic qualities that make humans a unique species are positive and drawn from a higher state.

The ability to care, and thus create quality – to act with courage in the face of fear – to hope, dream and use our imagination in the face of despair – to give and thus love in the presence of hate – this is the essence of our human nature.

117

Others have accused me, of being far too strict in my analysis. The concept of integrity and honor that I proposed are too rigid, and should be relaxed depending upon the circumstances. In other words, we need one standard of conduct for family, another for friends, and another still for strangers. Once someone said there is nothing more self righteous then a reformed whore. I suppose I am that reformed whore. When different standards are invoked for various circumstances, even if no one is victimized, we, nevertheless, injure ourselves. Our values must be constant. We are here to live with integrity and quality, even if no one outside of our self accepts that fact. What then is this failure's guide to a successful life?

First, recognize the reality of pain and suffering in our life. It is the way of our existence. The reality of the pain, or the perceived threat of the pain, will trigger the deep responses from our limbic system. Flight or fight instincts will flow to the forefront. Not only must we recognize the pain of life, the suffering must be embraced, even welcomed as the reality of our existence. How can we hope to face reality, unless we can deal with the pain and difficulty of life?

A very young Paul Newman portrayed the role of boxing champion Rocky Graziano in the movie Somebody Up There Likes Me. Barred from fighting in his hometown of New York, because of his past military criminal record, Graziano's championship fight was transferred to Chicago. Our hero was uncomfortable with the surroundings, and the night before the fight he flew back to his old neighborhood to reminisce. Soon he found himself in his old hangout, an ice cream parlor. Immediately, Graziano began complaining about the fans in Chicago and all the evils that had befallen him. In response, the owner offered his view of life. Pointing to the ice cream soda that Rocky had ordered, the older man said that life was like that soda. You order the soda and I give you a check. If you want the soda you have to pay the check. You can't have the soda without paying the check, he summarized. Armed with this little piece of Hollywood logic, Rocky proceeded to defeat Tony Zale the next evening.

Life presents us with a check for everything. Often that check involves sacrifice, denial, and hard work. Rarely, if ever, does the check presented by life involve unending pleasure. How then to deal with the pain? First, act always to deny instant gratification for a purpose. Know that the short term pain will produce long term gain. Then create a system of integrity and quality in all you do. Use the valuable emotional system we have as an asset not a liability. Take our rational ability and merge it with our emotions by wrapping both functions with a spirit of integrity and enthusiasm. This creates a synergy that makes us better the sum of the parts.

Beware the feel good tendencies inherent in ideas such as self-love, self-image and self-esteem. Strive, instead, to formulate a deep sense of self worth that will help in creating quality while serving as armor against the slings of others. When faced with the difficulties of life, of course, assume a positive mental attitude. But that mental approach will be based upon the bedrock of worth, and not the flights of unbridled optimism.

Under no circumstance permit your life to be validated by the acceptance of others, or by the number of material things you accumulate. Acquire the most beautiful possession, if you choose. Be accepted by all, as long as that acceptance does not create who you are, but serves as a compliment to a vital, integral person of self worth and quality.

By all means, take prudent risks. To risk failure is necessary. But the watchword is prudent. Draw upon the truly human qualities of caring, quality, courage, hope, imagination, and perseverance. Purge your system with tears or laughter when warranted. Recognize the importance of love and relationships, as essential to our human nature. Understand that the way of our existence is replete with randomness and chaos, and in spite of all our efforts mistakes will be made. Even if failure follows, the bedrock of your integrity and the depth of your self – worth will see you through the trouble.

My brother Michael provides just such an example. Along with a partner, he operated a medium sized beverage business. The hours were long and hard. The financial pressures were immense. But the operation was a success. Suddenly because of several economic factors the business closed. Stripped from my brother was his child, so to speak. To a small businessperson, that entity so carefully built is similar to a child. To a lesser person the loss would have been devastating. My brother, though, is just such a person of integrity and quality. Ironically, even the failure became a testament to his success. No one questioned what happened. His personal integrity would not permit such an inquiry. His depth allowed him to navigate for many months the randomness and chaos that followed the business loss.

And finally, above all take the time to ponder the mysteries of our universe.

So much for my lecture on the proper path of life. There is only one other realization that I wish to share with you. As I look back with mourning on all my failures, I am struck with another cliché – that we have only one life. Please, do it right.

**If you have any comments on the contents
of these essays, please e-mail the author at**
frank@franklyspeaking.cc

**Visit the website for other articles of interest
And public speaking availability**
www.franklyspeaking.cc

Printed in the United States
101888LV00001B/46-78/A